CAREERS
FOR
MUSIC
LOVERS
& Other
Tuneful Types

CAREERS

FOR

MUSIC
LOVERS

& Other
Tuneful Types

Jeff Johnson

VGM Career Horizons
a division of *NTC Publishing Group*
Lincolnwood, Illinois USA

Library of Congress Cataloging-in-Publication Data

Johnson, Jeff, 1965–
    Careers for music lovers and other tuneful types / by Jeff Johnson.
      p. cm.
    Includes bibliographical references.
    ISBN 0-8442-4340-X (hardcover : alk. paper). -- ISBN 0-8442-4341-8
(pbk. : alk. paper)
    1. Music trade--Vocational guidance. I. Title.
    ML3790.J65 1997
    780'.23'73--dc20   916-26009
                                                CIP
                                                MN

Published by VGM Career Horizons, a division of NTC Publishing Group
4255 West Touhy Avenue
Lincolnwood (Chicago), Illinois 60646-1975, U.S.A.
© 1997 by NTC Publishing Group. All rights reserved.
No part of this book may be reproduced, stored in a retrieval system,
or transmitted in any form or by any means, electronic, mechanical,
photocopying, recording, or otherwise, without the prior permission
of NTC Publishing Group.
Manufactured in the United States of America.

    6 7 8 9 0 VP 9 8 7 6 5 4 3 2 1

Contents

About the Author

J eff Johnson serves as managing director of Interhit Records —one of the hottest new independent labels on the dance music scene. Jeff, along with his partner Chris Cox, formed Interhit Records in 1994. Interhit has since gone on to great success with its *DMA Dance* compilation series and hits from artists, including Outta Control, Alexia Phillips, Linda Imperial, and Jeff Johnson himself. Previous to running Interhit Records, Jeff spent six years as a member of the Warner Bros. Records promotion team and was involved closely with the promotion of countless records by hit artists, including Madonna, Prince, Rod Stewart, and REM, among others. In addition to his current position as managing director of Interhit, Jeff Johnson also serves as assistant editor for *DMA* magazine where he has interviewed artists such as Donna Summer, Gloria Estefan, Pet Shop Boys, Diana Ross, Ace of Base, and many others for *DMA* cover stories. In addition to his writing duties at *DMA*, Jeff has written or cowritten ten books, including *Careers for Music Lovers*. Jeff graduated Phi Beta Kappa with Honors in English from Northwestern University.

This book is dedicated to my parents
for believing in me

CHAPTER ONE

A&R: Artists & Repertoire

The A&R department is the "ears" of the record company. A&R stands for Artists and Repertoire. In other words, A&R people concern themselves with finding artists for the record label and finding the proper material—or repertoire—for those artists to record. This department listens to bands, musicians, and singers and also reviews demo tapes and records released on independent labels. A&R people act as talent scouts. They seek out the next rising music stars and attempt to sign them to recording contracts before the competition does. The best A&R people are the ones with the best ears. In other words, they are the ones who can hear the hits of tomorrow—who can spot the stars-to-be, who can develop and nurture the next generation of successful artists. If you feel that you have a good ear, a desire to work with artists, and the ability to spend long hours in the studio, at clubs, and on the road, then by all means look into the field of A&R. A&R can be an exciting, demanding, challenging, and cut-throat field. The competition between A&R people at the major-label level is quite intense. Only those with a great ability to hear and predict what will be successful in the future should consider this career path. The turnover in this field is great. Keeping your job depends on whether or not the artists you sign to the label are successful. One major success can secure your position at the company for many years. A bad patch of signings can lead to termination. Often entire A&R staffs are let go when the head of the department is replaced for whatever reason. It can be a volatile field, so be forewarned.

A&R definitely falls on the creative side of the music business. A good A&R person is able to make the right decisions regarding an artist's career, from the signing of that artist to the selection of songs for albums, even to the look and image of the artist, from photos to music videos. Often, after signing an artist, the A&R person shepherds that artist's career at the record label and makes sure that the artist gets the proper attention and treatment from the rest of the company. Sometimes an A&R person is also a record producer and consequently becomes even more involved in the creative development of an artist than the traditional A&R person. At Warner Bros. Records, A&R Vice-President Ted Templeman, besides signing and developing artists, has enjoyed a successful career as a record producer and is responsible for production on several albums by Van Halen and The Doobie Brothers. Besides signing the massively successful punk group Green Day, A&R Director Rob Cavallo also produced their Reprise Records debut album, which sold over nine million copies. The right A&R staff can mean the difference between success and failure for a record company. Unfortunately, during bad times, the A&R people are the first to go!

Marc Nathan, Vice-President of A&R

A veteran of the A&R game who can boast successful signings at both Atlantic Records and the newly formed MCA label—Universal Records—is Marc Nathan. Marc gives us the inside story on the field of A&R from his office in New York.

Q: How did you break into the business?

"I was fifteen years old, living in Queens, New York. I wrote a fan letter to Todd Rundgren, who had just released his first album, *Runt*. About three weeks later, shortly after my sixteenth birthday, I received a reply from the head of promotion at Ampex Records, the label that Todd recorded for. I was so jazzed about getting a letter and a free record from this guy that I went into Manhattan, went up to the record company, hung out, and at the end of the day I asked if they needed any help. They said they could use someone packing 'those records over there, in these envelopes over here.' I went back the next day and typed up a mailing list of labels. By the third day they said, 'Kid, you never shut up,' so they gave me a list of reporting radio stations and told me to call them, asking music directors for their opinion on the new Todd Rundgren single. I did that, and the next thing I knew, I was a promotion man! I was going to Forest Hills High School at the time and I was on a split session so that I was out by noon. I took the subway into the city and worked a full eight-hour shift at the record company. I graduated high school in the spring of 1972. At the age of seventeen I had already been doing radio promotion for almost a full year. At that point, I enrolled in New York University and was there for five days. On the fifth day, I realized that when the professors would say, 'Okay class, take a ten-minute break,' I was running downstairs to a pay phone to call Top-40 stations in Minnesota and North Dakota to find out if they were adding my records. So I dropped out of college and became a full-time promotion man. I did promotion from late 1971 through 1988.

"Basically I was lucky, having grown up in New York City and having a passion for the music from as early as I could remember. My father was a bass player in a band in the fifties; my grandmother had sung on the radio in the thirties. I was very fortunate to be eight years old when the Beatles first started their invasion of the United States. I was very actively aware of rock and roll music and Top-40 radio. I was a subscriber to both *Record World* and *Billboard* when I was twelve years old. I was aware of how radio stations worked and, like so many other kids, I would buy records and do my own Top-40 chart in a little spiral notebook every week. I would sit on my bedroom floor and pretend I was a disc jockey. When I was sixteen and in the record business and dealing with radio people, I realized that if I had grown up in a small market, say in North Dakota or West Virginia or Tennessee, I would have been the sixteen-year-old kid hanging around the Top-40 station who might have gotten a chance to do overnights on the radio. Then, instead of being the child prodigy in the record business, I would have been the child prodigy in radio. It's just that I had a passion for it and maneuvered myself into a position where I made myself indispensable at the label. I was very, very grateful for the opportunity and fortunate to seize it."

Q: How did you get into A&R?

"In 1988, having done radio promotion for the better part of eighteen years, I was on vacation in Toronto, Ontario, and was in a dance club. A record started playing that really perked up my ears. I yelled up to the deejay asking him the name of it because it literally took all of five notes for me to be sure that I was hearing a hit record, and one that I had never heard before. He told me that the artist was Kon Kan, and the song was called "I Beg Your Pardon." In fact, the deejay spinning the record was the act! I went to the record store the next day, and the deejay, who was the artist, was also a clerk at the store. The record was pressed on a small independent label in Toronto. I bought seven copies of the record and flew back to New York City. I gave one copy to the president of Atlantic Records, one to the head of A&R, and sent the other five to different radio stations I believed would give it a fair listen. The five radio stations added the record, the president of Atlantic Records raised an eyebrow, and the head of A&R basically ignored me because I was in promotion and it was not my job. But, when the record started to get reaction at the radio stations, Atlantic signed the act and, of course, we went on to have a world-wide smash. My reward was that I got the opportunity to do

A&R. It was really a fluke of sorts. I was looking for a way to change my career path because after eighteen years of doing the same job, I admit that I had become a little disenchanted with the daily grind of radio promotion and trying to come up with the edge that would get my records on the radio before the next guy's records. By signing a hit record, I had my calling card into the A&R world.

"Subsequently, I signed three other songs at Atlantic that went Top-10 in different genres. I didn't sign any huge artists, but I signed hit records. Within a year of doing A&R, I had a Top-10 rhythm-and-blues record with a song called "Babies Having Babies" by Terry Tate. I had the number-one dance record with Kon Kan. I had a Top-5 single and a pretty good-sized album with Linear and Linear's hit, "Sending All My Love." My last signing was an alternative act called King Missile. The album that I executive produced with them, *The Way to Salvation*, was in the Top-10 on college and alternative tip sheets for the better part of six months."

Q: And then what happened?

"I tried to sign an artist that I personally believed in to the point of obsession. Nobody at the company shared my obsession and I was asked to take my ball and go home. Basically, the relationship that I had with Doug Morris, the president of Atlantic Records, was different than most employer/employee relationships because he had also been at Ampex Records in 1971 and so had known me since I was sixteen, spanning a good portion of my childhood and all of my adult life. We were very, very close, but he was the boss and, to be honest, I admit that at times I forgot that. Because I had known him so long and I acted inappropriately, I was relieved of my duties. At that point in time, I decided to venture into personal management. I managed a handful of artists over the next couple of years. Management is very tough unless you have an act that can generate steady income.

"Now I'm back in A&R—and working for Doug Morris, which is the beauty of the whole thing. People didn't necessarily understand how Doug could bring me back after he had fired me. I put in eight years at Atlantic Records working for him and then got fired. It was a shock to many people in the Atlantic camp. But then, to be the first person that Doug hired when he was putting together his new team at Universal came as an even bigger shock to many of the same people. It might even have come as a shock to me, except that I exhibited a certain level of humility, coupled with the willingness to understand that he is the boss. I know how Doug Morris works and what he looks for. So, my job in A&R here isn't that of a traditional A&R person. I am more his secret weapon—though I guess it's not so secret if I'm telling my story in a book. I'm his research guy within the A&R department.

"To break that down more specifically, there are a number of artists who will self-produce their own records and release them through small independent labels. It's my job to find the ones that break beyond the fan base and become real hits. Over the past few years, Doug was very successful at that—finding acts like Hootie and the Blowfish in the Carolinas, Collective Soul down in Gainesville, Florida, All-4-One, and a few others. It's a tried-and-tested method that will virtually always work for you—if you are doing your homework and making sure you are reading beyond the hype. When you find something in a small market and it's selling beyond its core audience—meaning the record does better than just getting sold at the concert or on consignment in quantities of one and two at a local record store. When a thirty-five-year-old housewife calls a radio station to ask about a particular record, not even knowing that it's a local act, or when a radio station plays a record that reacts as positively as a major hit record on a major label and it's not just the band members' relatives calling to request it, you know you have the makings of a hit record. These records are difficult to find, and what makes me unique is probably the fact that I have twenty-five years worth of experience—I've been on the promotion side of the fence, I've been on the management side of the fence, and I've been on the A&R side. So, unlike a typical A&R guy who just says, 'I trust my ears and I love it and I want to make a record with these people,' I can walk into Doug Morris and say, 'I found this record, it sold six thousand copies out of Lansing, Flint, and Kalamazoo, and now the radio station in Detroit is starting to pick it up. And, before they do, I think we better pick it up because it's going to sell fifty thousand in Detroit and then we'll be able to spread it to Cleveland and Pittsburgh within ten minutes.'"

Q: What skills and/or education does one need to make it in A&R?

"Well, normally you would say you have to have good ears, but my boss would throw that theory out the window. You're only as good as your last hit, and there are very few A&R people who consistently have 'that magic touch.' In some ways, I think that Doug Morris is one of the few people who has it because he's had an uncanny ability to come up with hit after hit throughout his lengthy career in the industry. He even wrote a major song himself, ('Sweet Talking Guy' for the Chiffons back in the early sixties), so he's a man who's been associated with hits all his life. I don't mean to downgrade their place within the industry in any way, but A&R is so purely subjective. You never really know where the next big hit is going to come from, and the person who finds that next big hit may not find anything else for the rest of their lives.

"Early in my A&R career, I had the ability to find hit records, but not hit acts. When push comes to shove and you are dealing with the bottom line of dollars and cents, I would much rather find a hit artist than someone who is only going to deliver one single and never be heard from again. As far as education goes, I guess I'm personally living proof that it didn't take a college education to carve out a career. However, I think that given the chance to do things a little differently, I might have figured out a way to make more time in my life schedule for classes in advertising and marketing and various and sundry communications classes because it could have only made me more well rounded. Most things I picked up on the fly because my education was on-the-job training."

Q: What do you like most about your job?

"I like the fact that after all these years I still have this incredible passion for the music. When I was in promotion, not all of the records that I really had a passion for became hits, so it was very difficult for me to be able to channel my energies into something that I didn't personally believe in. With A&R, you have opportunities in your life to work with artists you really believe in. King Missile may have never sold one-tenth of the records that a group like Linear sold on its hit or Kon Kan sold on its hit, but I gained personal satisfaction having been involved with a guy like John S. Hall, who later on went on to write some timeless songs. I think that's a tremendous feather in my cap—to be able to say that I helped bring that music to the general public. I would love to be involved with signing things that really mean something to people."

Q: What is the most challenging aspect of your job?

"Definitely weeding out the hype from the reality. We're in a situation where we have many, many research tools at our fingertips, but you really have to have an incredible feel for how to read the research. A record can sell a whole lot of records; stores can tell you that it's blowing out in sales and getting tons of requests; radio stations can tell you that they're playing it thirty times a week and it's absolutely a hit record, but it's really challenging to figure out which are really going to make it and go all the way and which are just going to sit there and be local phenomena."

Q: What advice would you give someone who wants to get into A&R?

"Have passion and most importantly don't believe that you have all the answers. We can all name three or four records in our collections that we fell in love with that didn't become national hits. It's very easy to say, 'Boy, the record company really missed it on that one.' But, the fact is, if the record company made it available to the public and the public didn't bite, then it probably wasn't really a hit. Hits are few and far between. Trust your instincts to a point, but as soon as it's proven that something really isn't as big as you want it to be, just let it go. There will always be another one."

Art Design

T he look and image of the artists is almost as important as their music. Often a tasteful and striking CD cover can catch the consumer's eye in a record store and possibly interest that consumer in listening to and buying that record. In the age of MTV, the importance of the visual cannot be overlooked. Often artists gain respect because of the uniqueness of the artwork on their records or in their advertising. The responsibility for the look of a record's package falls under the talented eye of the record company's art designer. For those with a talent and an interest in art and in music, a career as an art designer or graphic artist for a record company may be the right path.

Designing the art for a record is one of the most creative jobs in the music business next to actually being a recording artist. The art designer gets to create a visual representation of what he or she feels the artist's newest music reflects or inspires. Each record album represents a new phase in a recording artist's career, and this career is ever evolving, growing, and changing. The artwork must reflect that growth and change, hence the art designer's role in helping to mold the recording artist's visual presentation to the public is immeasurable. Sometimes the art designer works with traditional methods when creating the artwork, but usually the entire design is generated on a computer. So a knowledge of computer graphics and art becomes indispensable for those working in the record industry. Another exciting part of the job of art designer is interaction with the artists themselves and the thrill of helping to shape a recording artist's vision through the medium of art.

Another equally important position on the artistic side of the recording industry is that of graphic artist. The graphic artist produces advertising layouts, posters, stickers, flyers—anything that needs to be generated graphically at a record label. The work of a graphic artist involves more manipulation of already existing art than creation of new images and artwork. A graphic artist may take the artwork from an album and enlarge it for a full-page ad in a magazine and lay text on top that tells of the latest sale figures and chart numbers for that artist. A graphic artist may take a photo of a band and create a T-shirt that is in turn sold at concerts or given away through contests. Thus, a graphic artist may be more involved with the marketing of a recording artist than the art designer. The graphic artist contributes equally with the art designer to the successful visual presentation of the recording artist.

Tom Recchion, Executive Artist and Multimedia Director

Tom Recchion is the executive artist and multimedia director for Warner Bros. Records and has created artwork for albums by countless Warner Bros. artists. Tom had these insights for those interested in a career in art in the music business.

Q: How did you break into the business?

"Originally I utilized connections that I had made in art school by getting into any kind of graphics work that I could find. From there I met someone who knew an art director at Warner Bros. When I lost my job at the magazine that I was working at, I contacted one of the Warner Bros. art directors. I had a good recommendation from a previous employer, so they let me come by to do some production work. This was a long time ago, before computers were part of the job. What I would recommend to people now is to try and get into an intern program and to make sure that they learn as many computer programs as possible, at least on the graphics end of things. An intern program is a really good opportunity, and certainly cold calls don't hurt either."

Q: Did you find it hard to get into a major record label?

"I didn't. I found it quite simple, actually. Surprisingly so. That was the first time I had worked at Warner Bros., and then I went away for a couple of years and worked at other publications and pursued my music. When I decided that I wasn't going to make my living doing music, I went back to Warner Bros. and asked if I could some free-lance work. Because I had had previous experience there, they said sure. They appreciated that I knew the system. I worked at home for a couple of months doing free-lance work, and then I filled in for different designers and art directors on vacation. Then they asked me to come in on a permanent free-lance basis, and eventually I was offered an entry-level position at the very bottom rung of the ladder, as they say, and from there I worked my way up."

Q: What skills and/or education are needed in the art side of the record business?

"I think the skills you need are really the desire to do the work, some creativity, and a desire to try new things. I had a very unusual career. I didn't study graphic design. I went to a fine arts school and studied drawing and video tape. I got into graphics through connections I had made in art school because people who I went to school with were doing free-lance graphics and making pretty good money doing that. I had been working in every level of the record business, retail and wholesale—everything from starting off as a clerk in a record store to managing record stores to then managing record distributors.

Then I realized that I was interested more in art than in business, so I started to pursue that more aggressively.

"For me, getting into graphics became a matter of making money to support my music. So my career is an odd one. It's an odd example. There are a lot of people who study design and they know that's what they want to do. For me that wasn't the case. I had done design work for myself and for friends. As a visual artist I had a penchant for it.

"I love music and I do think I know what interests me in terms of graphics for a package. I think the person has to have the right sensitivity to it. If you're working in-house for a major record label, you're given a variety of projects. You have to be able to move in and out of different styles comfortably because one style may not fit the next artist. I think a person interested in this career has to have a lot of sensitivity to music and a lot of desire to work in that field. It's very different from designing a magazine or designing an annual report. You can approach it on a lot of levels. You can approach it at the level of pushing your style onto a project, or you can come up with something that may not be purely indicative of your sensitivities or your sensibilities, but it's something you arrive at in collaboration with a particular artist. There's an array of approaches that come to play when you're working with a large rock group with several different musicians."

Q: What exactly do you do in your job?

"I administrate the department in every facet and I do that in collaboration with Janet. Janet and I co-run the department. It's our responsibility to assign projects to different art directors. We find out what records are coming out, and then we make the assignments. We strive to make assignments with some degree of sensitivity. We know that if it's a heavy metal act, we're not going to give it to somebody who designs primarily jazz projects. We administer the department in terms of hiring, firing, and promotions. We're responsible for budgets.

"Our main responsibility, though, is the visual presentation of the company—how Warner Bros. records is represented visually. And we are still acting as art directors and designers ourselves. When we do that, our responsibility—and every art director's responsibility—is to start at the beginning phase, the concept phase, where we meet with an artist and discuss the project, their music, and we see if they have any ideas or feelings about how they would like their music represented. Then we decide whether or not it's going to be a photograph or an illustration or both. We find the photographers or illustrators to develop the concept, and then we make a presentation to the artist and management. We organize photo sessions, do the photo sessions, and then do the final design, including all typographic approaches. Sometimes with the computer we get into a lot of image and type manipulations because the variables are so vast when computers come into play."

Q: What do you like most and least about your job?

"I like designing best, and what I find most challenging about the job is the administration end of it. It is the most complex aspect of the job. I want to be a good employer. I want to treat people fairly and I want people to be happy in their jobs and that's a lot of work."

Q: What advice would you give about getting into art in the record industry?

"I think I would advise them to pursue it with a passion. Be tenacious and hang in there. If there's an opportunity to get into a record company, take it no matter what level it's at because people come and go in departments and there is generally a way to work your way up. But I think tenacity always pays off in whatever you choose to do."

CHAPTER THREE

Artist Development

A nother important division of a record company is artist development. Sometimes called product management, the artist development department serves as the
liaison between the artist and the record company. The product manager is the record label's "point man" for the artist and
the artist's manager—he or she makes sure the artist's needs
from the label are addressed properly and in a timely manner.
If an artist's manager needs to know what's going on with radio promotion on the new single, with those T-shirts from merchandising, with that tour advance from accounting, with the
release date information from scheduling—all he or she needs
to do is to contact the product manager—the primary contact
person in artist development. It's the product manager's job to
go to promotion, merchandising, accounting, and scheduling
and find these things out. Since the product manager works and
interacts day-to-day with many of the record label's departments, it's far easier for the product manager to get information from the label than it would be for the artist or the artist's
manager. Often, the product manager is supplied with regular
reports from other departments, so that he or she can have this
information readily available at all times. The product manager
has the truest overall picture of what is going on with a particular artist at that label. Artist managers can't attend most record
company meetings, but the product manager can and ultimately
has the best idea of what's happening at any particular time
with a particular artist.

A career in artist development can be an enjoyable experience for people who like dealing daily with creative people,

working out problems, and seeing their work come to fruition with the success of one of their artists. A product manager is often there at the beginning of a successful artist's rise to fame. It can be a thrilling and gratifying ride, knowing that you had something to do with another's success.

Eric Fritschi, Product Manager

Eric Fritschi, product manager for Reprise Records, has worked his way up the label ladder into the world of artist development. Eric talks about how he got started in the business only a few years back and gives us the unique perspective of someone who had little experience in the beginning but who worked hard, persevered, and got what he wanted—a job as product manager at a major record label.

Q: How did you get into the record business?

"I moved myself out to Hollywood, California, from Cincinnati, Ohio. I temped for a long time—in a lot of different industries, doing regular jobs. Eventually, I started working at film studios and the like, but I always wanted to work at a record company and I ended up at Warner Bros. Records in the summer of '92 as a temp. I didn't have much to do as a temp, so I organized the CD cabinets and called radio stations and requested that they play our records. I became the official temp of promotion. One day I worked in publicity, but the promotion department called me out at noon because they needed me in promotion right away! Temping was a lot of fun. You could take records home for free. What a dream that was. I wanted to take all of them home and listen to them.

"Then my job came up in contemporary music and I couldn't have asked for more in a job. I had a boss who was really on top of things, had a lot of great ideas, and had his hand in everything in terms of rock promotion, college promotion, dance promotion, production, remix production, scheduling, conventions. If it existed, somehow he had a hand in it. He took four months to hire me, and the day he called me in for my *fourth* interview, I sat in his office and he asked me, 'So, do you want the job?' I took two weeks' vacation and started full-time in July of 1992. You have to know somebody to get into this business and, if you don't know anybody, you have to meet them. There are many ways to meet them—even working as a temp and being the lowest person on the totem pole is a great way to meet people, from vice-presidents on down. You're their assistant. You get to know them well, and that's how I got to know the people I needed to know to get my job. I was one step ahead of the interns. Because they aren't getting paid, they don't have the same kind of clout or respect that you get if you come in and you're getting paid every day and clocking in and out.

"I stayed in that job for three years. The job was always growing. I had the same job title the whole time—department coordinator and assistant to the vice-president—but the job itself kept changing. I got a second assistant to help out. While I was there I did all the advertising and promotions, independent promotion, all the bills for a while. I planned conventions. And I kept learning new things. I handled all the dance video remixes. It was good, but eventually I felt it was time to move up. I was actually getting ready to leave at the time and I got really lucky. The contemporary music department disbanded and my boss, Craig Kostich, was heading a new department in an area I had always wanted to work in: artist development. I wanted to work with every aspect. I wanted to work on artists rather than on singles. I wanted to deal with all aspects of the artist's career, not just what radio stations were interested in, or what dance clubs were interested in, or what we wanted to advertise, but every little thing. I wanted to interact with the artists. In promotion, we didn't interact with the artists unless they were in town and we went to the show and did the 'Dog

& Pony Show'—we went by, we said hello, and they didn't know your name two minutes later. I wanted to be there with the music. Hearing the new Madonna record four months before anybody else was so exciting. Being close to the music was one of the reasons I had joined the company, and the other was to actually work with musicians and artists. So, when Craig jumped into artist development and was heading the department, I knew that this was an area that I wanted to be in and, after some haranguing, I got my shot to try it out. I got two artists—Poster Children and The Barenaked Ladies."

Q: How did you like it when you were finally doing it?

"It was like a dream come true. It was so awesome. Especially with Poster Children. The Barenaked Ladies are a bigger act and their record was over at that time. They were finishing up their tour. There was nothing to do really, but go say 'hi' and try to convince them that I was going to be important to their career one day. But with Poster Children, they had had a first single that didn't really happen, and then I came in and paid attention to them and that was so new to them—the fact that somebody cared on a daily basis about them at the label. So, together we all came up with a lot of new ideas for the group. When you work with artists at that level in their career, you can try out a lot of things without having a lot of people watch you. Things that you can't try on a Green Day, you can try on a Poster Children.

"Soon enough the other product managers became overloaded and there were a lot of unassigned bands, so I started to get a couple more bands, and all of a sudden I'm a product manager responsible for fifteen bands. They're all in different stages. Some of them have their records finishing and we're wrapping things up and making sure everything happens, and there's a whole bunch that aren't going to have records yet. There's one band that's not going to have a record for a year, but we're trying to develop it to a point where we can put a record out there, a successful one. Several have records coming out right now and we have to make sure their set-up is in place and that everything's right."

Q: Why does a record label need an artist development department?

"Small labels might not need one because there are fewer people involved and you have managers that perform the function of an artist development person, but for a label like Reprise, there are a lot of people—a lot of artists and a lot of managers. We're such a big system that it's hard to learn. A lot of artists and their managers don't know our system very well, and rather than wait for particular managers and artists to learn the system, we come pre-programmed. We are like their nanny. We already know our system very well and can do what's right for the artist. All we do, really, is facilitate thing, make things happen. The promotion function works as it would anywhere else, as do the publicity, sales, and merchandising functions. But when you have an artist roster of sixty to eighty artists, it's hard for each of those people to keep up with every one of those artists. It's hard enough for me to take care of the fifteen artists that I take care of, but I can do a better job of that than somebody watching over sixty artists. The artist development department is needed because we look after the artists, we make sure that we're doing the right things, and we get a truer picture of what's going on than a manager would because we're there every day and other departments at the label have to deal with us every day. I know what other departments are doing and what they're not doing. I'm also allowed to know the reality on other artists. Other departments don't have to hide things from me. Managers wouldn't know what's happening with other artists because it's confidential information, but I am privy to sales numbers and meetings that managers don't get in on."

Q: What advice would you give to someone wanting to break into this business?

"I know my scenario the best, but if I had advice for anybody I would say get involved as soon as you can. As soon as you know that this is going to be your interest, get involved in whatever you can—working at your college radio station, writing for your school newspaper about music, or helping to book bands on your campus or at the local club. Anything you can do will help you immeasurably. It will at least give you a starting point to see what it's really like. Work in a record store. I worked in a record store when I first started for a long time, and that gives you a perspective on how things work and insight for when you actually work at a record company and you're shut off from a lot of things. And once you graduate, once you've hopefully done some of those things, you've got to go to one of the music centers. The easiest ones are New York and Los Angeles. Meet people. You need to know people to get in. Realize you're going to start on the bottom. You're going to need to know people to actually even get in at the bottom. Don't think that because you have a university degree you're going to start as some sort of manager and have a quick key to the executive washroom. Temping is a great way to get started; interning, if you're still in school, is a good way; being at shows, checking out the bands, checking out the music are good ways. To be in artist development, you need to try to understand all the different aspects of working in this business, so leave yourself open to everything. Check out all the magazines you can. Check out all the record stores you can. Listen to as many radio stations as you can in different markets, and when it comes down to it, find people you want to work with and get closer to them."

CHAPTER FOUR

Record Promotion

ebster defines promotion as "to make aware." That's what record promotion is all about. The promoter's job is to make the record-buying public aware of the record that he or she is promoting. The way record promoters do this is by getting their records played on radio stations across the country. The more radio airplay—the more records sold. Period. Airplay sells records. Hence, the importance of the record promoter and the promotion department at a record company. A radio hit can make the difference between a few thousand albums sold and hundreds of thousands of albums sold. More often than not, those who succeed in the field of promotion go on to run record labels themselves.

The telephone is the record promoter's best friend—it's the instrument of choice, the one with which the promoter performs the magic of persuasion. Calling radio stations is the record promoter's primary responsibility. Promoters must be good persuaders and good networkers. They must be friendly, yet firm, in order to get results. Radio program directors (PDs) and music directors (MDs) decide weekly, usually on Tuesday, which records to add to their station's playlist. They usually set aside time before Tuesday when they accept calls from record label and independent promoters. This is the precious time that the promoter must use to work magic on the PDs and MDs. The competition for "adds" to each station's playlist is fierce, and the promoter must use, in addition to powers of persuasion, whatever hard evidence of the record's success at other stations or in record sales that he or she can find. If a record has been added by other stations, it becomes easier to convince a pro-grammer to "get on the bandwagon." If the record shows healthy sales in the particular station's marketplace, this also can help the promoter's cause. The record promoter needs a "story" to tell the radio programmers—in other words, success in other markets and areas. If you have a story, you may just get that coveted add.

The key research tools that the promoter uses to develop the story are Broadcast Data Systems (BDS) and SoundScan. BDS tracks, via computer, radio airplay on most key stations throughout the United States. BDS encodes each record on computer and in each important market, BDS computers moni-tor radio airplay twenty-four hours a day. By using "BDS Re-ports," record promoters can gauge the true national airplay picture for the records they are promoting. Before BDS, record labels had to rely on playlists reported by the radio stations themselves. At times, these playlists proved inaccurate as cer-tain radio stations became known for "paper adds"—adding a record and not actually playing it, resulting in an add only on paper. This practice became obsolete with the advent of BDS. No longer can a station add a record without playing it because BDS tracks everything the station plays twenty-four hours a day, seven days a week.

"SoundScan, which began in 1991, provides computer track-ing of sales based on bar-code scans at the cash register. Like BDS, SoundScan provides an accurate, though incomplete, picture of record sales across the country. Many record stores are equipped with a SoundScan system that tracks every sale at the register, but SoundScan doesn't tell the whole story be-cause many small independent retail outlets are not equipped with the costly SoundScan setup. Still, it is the most accurate estimate of sales and is used religiously throughout the record industry. Before SoundScan, sales charts were based on indi-vidual store sales charts, which at times proved inaccurate. An accurate SoundScan sales report gives record promoters ammunition with which to convince radio programmers to add their records. Since the SoundScan reports are divided by city, promoters can pinpoint sales "stories" in particular markets and use them to get adds. For example, they can argue "If this many people are buying this record in your marketplace, you should be playing this record!"

Another tool the promoters can use are special promotions. A CD giveaway on the air, tickets to the artist's concert, or a contest involving an artist can all help to demonstrate the label's commitment to a record and help to secure the add. This is where the record promoter can get a bit creative in order to come up with different special promotions for individual stations—maybe airfare and tickets to a Janet Jackson concert in London or a T-shirt giveaway at the local mall.

"In the end, though, the best tools record promoters have are their relationships with the radio programmers. A promoter has to be a "people person"—someone who can make friends and gain trust. A positive personal relationship with a radio programmer can be better than a truckload of BDS and SoundScan reports when it comes down to the wire on a Tuesday. Record promotion can be great fun and can provide a great deal of excitement and satisfaction in knowing that you had a hand in making a hit happen.

Ed Nuhfer, Promotion Director

One of the best record promoters in the business is Warner Bros. records promotion director Ed Nuhfer. Twenty-three years in the business of promotion makes Ed an expert on the subject. Here he explains the ups and downs of life as a major label record promoter.

Q: How did you break into the business?

"I came from sales and marketing. I was actually a salesperson on the road selling records and tapes to accounts. A job in promotion became available and the person who ran this company, which was a sales distributorship, thought that I would fit the bill, though I didn't really have a tremendous knowledge of what promotion people do other than that they were responsible for securing air play on radio stations. I was almost thrown into the job. I went in very, very green and asked advice of the person who hired me and also my predecessor. I developed the skills that were necessary to accomplish the task as I went along. Really, I came from a background of marketing—an area that gave me a deeper understanding of the needs and the wants of the consumer in the record marketplace than the needs of the radio listener, who the radio station has to address. However, at the time that I came into the business, a large part of what determined a successful record on a radio station were the sales of a record in a given marketplace, either because that radio station was playing the record already or there were other radio stations around it playing the record."

Q: What skills and/or education does one need to make it in record promotion?

"I think probably the issue that should be addressed first is education. Primarily, I think those who come from either a communications—journalism, writing—or a marketing background have a tendency to do better as promotion people. I've even known within this business many people who have either been in pre-law or in law school who have become very successful promotion people. My own education lies in communications. In terms of skills, you have to be a very good communicator. You also have to be a very good listener—not only able to listen to a radio station to understand what it is trying to accomplish on the air, but able to listen to the programming people at that radio station to determine what their needs are from a product standpoint. A record to a radio station is merely a utility—a commodity, a product used to make the radio station sound better, to advance its ratings. A promotion person's job—at least 85 to 90 percent of it—is to get records played on radio stations. That's it. There are other ancillary things that happen, but primarily the main goal is to get these records played so that they get listened to and so that the consumers will go out and buy the record if they like what they're hearing on the radio. But from a marketing standpoint you have to understand that the program directors are marketing their radio stations to the listeners. They want to give their listeners the environment that the listeners want to be in all the time. They want to keep the listeners listening to their radio station constantly, and they do that primarily through the music they play. So, being able to understand how they are attempting to market the radio station is important. You need to know exactly how to market your record. You cannot take, for example, a dance-oriented record and expect a rock-oriented radio station to play this record. You have to know the correct records and styles of music that go with a particular radio station in order to get them played. You have to understand what the radio station is trying to accomplish, and if you think you have that perfect record, then you need communication skills to explain this to the program directors. You have to be able to convince them that playing your record is going to benefit each particular station. More people will listen to their radio stations if they are playing the right record. People will listen longer. The ratings will go up. The station will be able to sell more advertising and charge more for this advertising and perhaps have more effective advertising because those listeners, in addition to going out and perhaps buying a record or two, will patronize the radio station's advertisers. So, understanding your market and understanding the radio station's market are the keys, as well as good communications skills."

Q: *What's the other 15 percent of your job?*

"In addition to getting records played on the radio, you also must wear several hats, including artist relations or artist development. To enhance the promotion job that you are doing by getting records played on the radio station, you must also create interest in your artists. In doing that you attempt to have program directors, music directors, and even retail record people—buyers of records at retail establishments and wholesale distributors—see the artist when the artist is on tour and giving a concert. Under the artist development part of your job, you take artists to radio stations, perhaps to conduct interviews to stimulate the listeners' interest in the artists or perhaps to encourage the listener to go to the show while the artists are on tour. By the same token, you can also do that in the print media—in national and local magazines, local newspapers. That's part of the job as well, albeit a smaller part compared to actually getting records played on the radio."

Q: *What do you like most about your job?*

"There are two things that I like about my job. The number one most likeable thing about my job is the music. I definitely like the music and I don't think I would be in this business if it weren't for the music. It seems that people in the music business, or in the recording business I should say, whether they are promotion people, marketing people, recording engineers, or whoever, are drawn to it because of the music. It's always the music, the music, the music.

"Second, I take a tremendous amount of delight in being able to work with an artist or a band that has never had a hit record before—being involved in helping this artist have a hit record. There is an ego gratifying part of watching the success of a band or an artist develop and knowing that you're part of it. Making the money for your company isn't bad, either.

"Third, there's the experience of being inside—not where the consumer is, not where anybody else is—being able to hear the music first, knowing the idiosyncrasies of the artists and their management, meeting them, working with them. That is pretty gratifying, too."

Q: What's the most challenging aspect of your job?

"Getting records played on the radio. The singularly most challenging part of the job, really, is securing the airplay for the artists because there are so many records released and so very, very, very, very, very few of them end up getting exposed. Each week there can be a group of about twenty-five records, or in some cases more, and I've seen it skew very high to as many as sixty or seventy records per week that a program director can choose to play or not play. And he may choose to play anywhere between one and four and in some cases more. Generally the number of records that get played is very, very small compared to the number that are actually being released. When you're able to secure that airplay you know that you at least have a chance to expose your artist to the consumers and, if the consumers happen to like what they're hearing, they take some money out of their wallets and go to the record store and buy that record."

Q: What advice would you give someone who wants to get into record promotion?

"Well, I would probably say that while you're in school you should definitely be working toward something that revolves around communications and/or marketing. Upon getting out of school or even before getting out of school, I would suggest that you apply for an internship with a label. Some labels actually have regional college representatives who call upon campus radio stations or go into record stores near college campuses to help market artists for the label by bringing in posters, perhaps even putting them up, that sort of thing. I think that that's a very, very good first step. Otherwise, good areas to get into as a precursor for becoming a promotion person would be taking a job at either a campus or a local radio station, either as a disc jockey or one of the programming people there, if you should be so lucky. Go to work in a retail record store and get to know the product and also the people who come into the store who represent the labels. Perhaps get a job with a distribution system and work your way up that way. Get a job as an assistant to a promotion person so that, through the day-to-day work, knowledge comes to you via osmosis. Those are some ways to get started. A large number of people in promotion today came from retail record stores, out of radio, out of wholesale sales, from positions as assistants to other promotion people. In every case, they picked up some of the knowledge of the business and developed their skills and eventually became promotion people."

CHAPTER FIVE

Publicity

A nother important department in the record company is the publicity department. Publicity handles all re-lations with the media regarding the label's artists. Sometimes this department is referred to as media relations, which describes its function more accurately. While the record promoter makes the public aware of particular songs, one of the most important aspects of promoting an artist is making the public aware of that artist. This is the job of the record company publicist. The publicist serves as the liaison between the label and the media and develops relationships and contacts with all relevant publications that can help to spread the word about a particular artist. These publications can include every-thing from local newspapers to national music magazines such as *Rolling Stone*, *Spin*, *Billboard*, *DMA*, and others.

Since many record companies are vying for media space, the competition for press coverage can be fierce. Publicists must use their communication skills, their relationship skills, and their promotion skills to land those coveted interviews, reviews, and concert coverage. The more people know about a certain art-ist, the more likely that artist's records are to sell. Before the release of a particular record, the publicity department is hard at work preparing press releases, writing bios, sending out ad-vance tapes to the press, and lining up interviews, reviews, and appearances. Publicity works closely with the artists and their managers in the early stages to insure proper media coverage of a record's release. The publicist must plan ahead and be pre-pared not to let any opportunity at media coverage pass by.

In addition to dealing with the press, the publicity department also arranges for TV and radio appearances for artists. Booking these appearances is often more of a challenge than landing press coverage. Artists, especially rock bands, tend to spend a lot of their time on the road touring. Many times, the publicist assigned to that band accompanies the artists on the road in order to escort them to any radio interviews or TV appearances that the record company may have arranged in any given city. If a band lands an appearance on national TV, you can bet that the record company publicist will be there to make sure that everything runs smoothly.

Ken Phillips, Publicist

One of the fastest-rising publicists in the Warner Bros. Records media relations department is Ken Phillips. Ken handles the publicity for several important Warner Bros. acts, including the Goo Goo Dolls, Joan Jett, the Red Hot Chili Peppers, and others. Ken discusses his road to success in media relations and the challenges of his job.

Q: How did you break into the business?

"I broke into the business working for a songwriter, basically doing personal assistant type work: running an office, music publishing, doing recording schedules, booking studio time, thinking of people to record songs for the songwriter, a little A&R in there. It was a little bit of everything but all music related."

Q: How did you get into publicity?

"I went to work for a temp agency, got placed at Warner Bros. Records, and started working in artist relations answering the phone. Then I got placed in publicity, answered the phones, and was hired a couple of weeks later. I basically became the receptionist for the whole department of eight publicists. I answered the phone, read tour and record release dates to journalists who called in, sent out bios and press kits, very minimal stuff. Then I worked for the senior vice-president of publicity, and little by little I acquired more responsibilities. I started doing tour press when bands went on tour, and then, after about a year or so, I started getting my own little acts to work on and the rest, as they say, is history."

Q: What do you do now?

"I have five or six acts of my own, and about three months before they have an album coming out, we sit down and talk about a publicity plan—what they want to target. It depends on what kind of band they are—if they're a band that can be on TV or if they're a band that only wants to concentrate on the college market or the mainstream market or the urban market. Then we do our advance mailings of the product that's coming out about three months ahead of time because that's about the right lead time for a magazine in order to get your reviews to come out at the same time as the album release. Then we have to start calling writers, telling them that the album is coming out, asking if they have any interest in interviewing the artists. Then we hire a photographer to do a photo shoot for the publicity shots and we have a writer who comes in and interviews the band for the bio. Then the album comes out and you hope it sells. And you get press and you get reviews and, providing the reviews are good, then you can use the reviews to help convince people to do bigger features on the band. Good reviews also help you to book the band on TV shows, which enables you to reach a broader audience. Hopefully it's a hit at radio because that's the most important thing—radio and MTV. Bigger and better things come on down the road if it's a hit. If it's not a hit, there are still critics who praise albums that don't ever get played on the radio, which can help a band's career. The Goo Goo Dolls had critical acclaim for so many years—great reviews, but they couldn't sell a record."

Q: What do you like most about your job?

"That it's something different every day. It's not always the same thing because each band that I work with is totally different. It's not a nine-to-five job. One day I could be on a photo shoot, the next I may be out on tour with an artist or on a video or TV shoot. You never know what's going to happen. It's just the spontaneity of it all."

Q: And what's the most challenging aspect of your job?

"I think it's trying to convince the writers that you have a band that's happening or that you know they should do a story on the band for whatever reason because it's so hard to convince writers to believe you unless they believe in the band already. It's really tough.

"And even when a band is successful, some writers don't always agree with you or with the success that they're having. So it doesn't mean that you're automatically going to get coverage simply because you have a band that has a Top-10 hit."

Q: What skills and/or education does one need to make it in publicity?

"I think a good dose of a psychology class. Just knowing people's personalities, being able to adapt to so many different kinds of people because you deal with a lot of creative people. Every single person is so different and sensitive and you have to be able to adapt to all different kinds of personalities and situations and really know where people are coming from.

"I would definitely take a psychology class, a communication or speech class, maybe even a journalism class, because there are a lot of times when you write press releases and pitch letters to writers and you want to be proficient. Those three things would probably be the most important. And also having ears— you've got to know about music, which is the most important part of publicity."

Q: What advice would you give someone who wants to get into your field?

"Go after what you want to do. Go to work for a record company and see how all the other departments run as well because you have to know that. It's not just the publicity part. Get an internship or work as a temp. If I were in college, I'd intern at a record company or work for the school newspaper to become familiar with how it all works. Definitely develop relationships with writers and with other publicists."

CHAPTER SIX

Sales and Marketing

A t a record company, the sales and marketing department has the responsibility of making sure that the company's product is available for sale in proper quantities in the marketplace. This department at a major label usually consists of sales representatives, sales managers, and sometimes branch managers. The sales and marketing department interacts with the distributor in order to maintain proper product flow, placement, sale pricing, retail promotion, and advertising—in other words, to make sure the product sells. Often the responsibilities of the sales and marketing department and those of the distributor overlap, depending on the size of the label. Those interested in a career in sales and marketing in the music industry should be outgoing, have a love of music, interact well with people, be persuasive, have a good sense of what's happening on the street, and love to sell. If this is you, you may one day experience the excitement of making a hit happen on the street.

The importance of a label having the product in the marketplace cannot be overemphasized. Timing is crucial in laying out a new release, and many a label has suffered the embarrassment of having a record on the radio and no product in the stores. Many young labels and artists look forward to the thrill of having their music played on the radio, but radio play without product in the marketplace can be a disaster. If people hear the record on the air and go to the store only to find they can't buy it—this is a lost sale—an unhappy situation for any salesperson.

The sales and marketing department begins its quest for that elusive million-seller by sending promotional copies of the label's new releases out to buyers at retail chains and independent record stores. Also included in this package is another crucial element—the "one sheet." The one sheet gives all possible relevant information on a new release, plus pricing, available configurations, bar codes, release dates, etc. The one sheet gives the buyer the basics and provides a forum for the sales and marketing department to hype the release. After listening and reading the one sheet, the buyer decides whether or not to order this particular release and how much to take in. Often the label's sales representative can influence a buyer to order more if that sales representative truly believes in the record's potential. A sales representative may be assigned a per-store allocation or a quota that the sales manager has set for a particular release. A sales representative must also be aware of the promotion, advertising, and publicity that the label has arranged. The efforts of other departments at the label often affect the way a sales representative sells to a particular market. If the promotion department has landed airplay in Seattle, the stores need to be well stocked there. If artist development has set up a big show in Memphis, the sales representative needs to make sure the product is in the stores there in time for the show. If the publicity department has set up a radio interview in Boston for an artist, the Boston rep should be aware of this and increase stock levels accordingly. This type of well-planned and perceptive interaction among departments at a record company can truly spur sales to higher levels.

Harvey Rosen, Sales Manager

A true veteran of the streets, Harvey Rosen, East Coast sales manager for MS Distributing Co., has done it all. From various sales and marketing positions at major labels—including sales representative, sales manager, director of sales and marketing, director of sales administration—to various high-level positions at large independent distribution companies, Harvey knows the business of selling records inside and out. In the following interview, he offers insight into the inner workings of the sales and marketing element of the record business and advice for those who want to break into this exciting field.

Q: How did you break into the business from a sales and marketing perspective?

"The true chronology is that, when I was selling stereo equipment and the company began to fail, a friend of mine invited me to interview because he was going back to work in the record industry. He had left Capitol Records after many, many years because they kept cutting the commission every time they had a bigger and bigger Beatles hit. He realized he really liked the industry and wanted to go back, and he wanted me to go back with him. He was going to go to RCA, where he knew, after a short time as a rep, he was going to be made branch manager because the branch manager and he were friends and the branch manager was going to become the regional manager. It was sort of a set up. I was instructed that if I wanted to get into the business, too, I should talk to the local branch manager for a job as rack jobber. I got in by being hired as a salesman in the middle Atlantic for both military and private-sector music departments at the racks, where I learned how records sell and how to mark and bring in all the records for all labels. I did the mid-shipment store at Annapolis, Dover Air Base, Woolworth, Woolco, Kresge's, and all of those grassroots locations where you put in your own 45s, you put in your albums, you wrote your own returns, you marked them to sale, you marked them down on sale and marked them back up and everything else for all labels.

"From there went to RCA when my friend did become the branch manager. So I started at RCA as a junior salesman in Baltimore/Washington, D.C., and then became a senior salesman in Manhattan, which got me back up into New York City. Then I went on to Polygram. After two years on the racks, Polygram saw the work I did and rather than have me compete against them, they felt it would be more advantageous to have me on their team. And I moved because I told them I was interested in becoming a sales manager someday. They said that if an opening occurred, I would get a shot at it.

"A year and a half after I left RCA and joined what was then called Phono Disc, which later became Polygram, I was actually given a chance as the New York assistant branch manager or sales manager. Then a year and a half after that, the D.C. branch opened and I moved down to Washington as branch manager for Polygram. Thirty-nine months later I came back to New York as the director of sales and marketing for Polygram's classical division, and the last couple of my ten years at Polygram were spent as director of sales administration—which is all the computers, all the commissions, all the prices, all the budgets, the data base, everything. I was referred to as Mr. Polygram because I was the guy who came up from the street and knew every level and every function of the company."

Q: *What skills and/or education does one need to make it in sales and marketing in the record business?*

"Education would be a difficult one to address. I really don't know. I think the skills you need are to be constantly using situations and opportunities that you see and using your prior experience to know how to employ those opportunities to create a sale. Basically the people who know what works rather than some theoretical program or theoretical idea or quota will succeed. Most of the people who are employed in the industry have, for some extensive period, been exposed to the way the product moves on the street. Generally those who don't succeed tend to either do things wrong or do them in a period of time or on a schedule that's simply not practical or assign quotas on how much product should be on the street in the first place that make no sense or are only driven by their corporate need to create billing. This is why they take back so many returns at the major labels because they don't know what to put out in the first place. They've never been out there to know and they don't listen to the people who are out there on the street."

Q: What does someone in sales at a record label do?

"Usually, if it's an independent label, that person speaks with the regional and local salespeople at the distributor to find out what can be done to work a record on the street. They coordinate what's going on with promotion and publicity to keep salespeople informed about things like tour support—if there's an artist's itinerary for a given area, for example—and try and work with them. By and large they make sure that people follow through. I mean our business is a business of relationships and follow through. If the sales manager at an independent label knows that the buyer for a given market is located a thousand miles away from the store he wants the records in, then he'll have some understanding as to what has to happen and who has to do it. At the majors, a label person is dealing with a branch manager more often than not and sometimes directly with the salespeople to accomplish the same thing, but it's the same company so there's some sort of a hierarchy and pecking order and protocol as to who is talking to whom about what. It's a lot more catch as catch can with the independent record labels."

Q: What did you like most about the job?

"Well, as a salesman, you're always in contact with the public and you're seeing what happens with people's buying patterns, which is probably the most important thing to know. As a sales manager, you're coordinating many salespeople and the various functions to effectively compete with other labels on the street. As a director of marketing, you're working with labels and artists at the next level up, the national level, to plan out what those strategies should be. Of course, if you've been on the street, probably you'll be more effective at knowing what works in which markets depending on the demographics of any given area. At the sales level, you're learning why people buy, when they buy and how they buy. For instance, most people—75 percent—buy music when they get paid, which is Thursday through Saturday. You'll learn that the best times to run your promotions, for instance in Washington, D.C., are biweekly because most people in the government and the military get paid biweekly toward the end of the week. If you don't know that, then you miss everything. If you do know that, you're very effective. On the sales management level, you get the benefits of still being connected to the street and becoming somewhat more knowledgeable in how top down management works and you meet some artists. At the national level, I guess the biggest thrill was to be able to do in-stores and attend concerts and dress rehearsals for people like Pavarotti and Pearlman and the Berlin Philharmonic, which I did. I had the opportunity to actually be one of the key people to introduce compact discs to various retailers and to the branch system at PGD, which was a lot of fun. And you travel a lot. There are a lot of different things that happen and at different levels as you move up."

Q: What was the most challenging aspect of those jobs?

"The most difficult thing is when you realize you have a staff for whom you are responsible. For instance, instead of only being responsible for yourself you have a staff of ten or twelve and now you have to cover some twenty or twenty-four weeks of vacation and their illnesses and their problems. Then you begin to learn that, if you tell a number of people the same thing, a percentage of them will do it right, but a significant percentage will not do everything, or will do some of it wrong. And so you're always prioritizing. Management is completely different than being a salesperson. You're responsible for the actions of others and you continuously have to delegate, follow through, double check, and collect results because you're not doing it yourself. You have to hope you can communicate what you want to others and that they follow up. You know that not everybody does everything. Everybody is very busy. It's a crazy business and priorities change every week and you have to keep some semblance of order in chaos."

Q: What advice would you give someone who wants to get into the record sales business?

"I think the most important thing is not just to read *Billboard* and think you know the record business. There are far too many people, especially at the larger companies, who make decisions and then delegate things to others without ever having the experience. It's not much different I think than the military, from what I've read, where somebody comes out of ROTC and they're a lieutenant and they have no real experience as a private, corporal, or sergeant. If you give orders to others without having received a basic training, as it were—where you know what goes on out there and how difficult it is—you won't be successful. I think that's to be avoided. I think many of our businesses in this country today are being run by people who come in with no experience, but they have the money and therefore the power and they tell people what to do and it's not practical, but the guy signs your check so you can't say anything. I think that the record business is very realistic, like life itself. If you don't know what's realistic in a given scenario, you're going to wind up frustrated and confrontational. A better understanding may not totally avoid that, but it would at least avoid an irresponsible or impractical goal or objective in either quantity or time. Everything is quantity and time. How much do you want and how fast do you want it. If you want something covered in two weeks and you don't know that there are a finite number of reps and a finite number of accounts and there are distances to be driven and appointments to be kept and it simply can't be done in three days, you're in trouble. Another problem is getting airplay before release. That's ridiculous. You don't get airplay before 80 percent of your accounts have had the opportunity to be covered with the product. 'I heard my record on the air and there's no records on the street.' Well, there couldn't be records on the street, but a lot of people simply have no idea that it takes three to five weeks to get records out because of all the realities of getting UPC numbers into everybody's system. If you don't have the experience of having done that, then you're not going to have a very high success quotient.

"So, I think my advice would be to try and get real world experience and not just ivory tower exposure—not just theoretical exposure on what the record business is about. It doesn't work that way. It can't work that way. No business can work that way, but especially music. It's very difficult to de-politicize the reality of sitting in a room and explaining to somebody you work for that he doesn't know what he's talking about because he's never been out there. When you visit a record store as a seller looking for seven or eight buyers at a given Tower store, you find how long and difficult and arduous it can be to get your priorities conveyed to other people and for them to respond because when you make your sale, it's usually before the record is a hit. The hard work is making the record available and prominent. My kids could sell a hit. A hit record didn't come out as a hit. There's no such thing. Records are developed into hits, that's the hard part and, if you don't know how, it's usually because you've never observed it, let alone attempted it. My focus has always been, 'Is what's being requested or discussed practical from all angles? And what are we up against and what else is going on out there and is the market difficult or is this the right week to do that and do the reps have the tools they need and the time they need to implement those tools.' Well, if you don't know what those things are, you're probably not going to score too high when it's time to make something into a reality by releasing it, getting it on the street, and working it up the ladder. So again, to a young person coming out of school, I would say hook onto a sales organization, even if it's for a short time, at the lowest level—the entry level or the sales level—and find out what it takes to cover all the Tower stores in Los Angeles before you think you're going to be able to tell a rep to do that in twenty-five minutes. Those are the things that most people don't know or they kind of know, but they've never really done it. They've never been there, so they really can't formulate a good strategy because their strategy is not based on the realities of time and distance and personnel and what else is going on out there. So, experience, not just book learning. In fact, experience is always the best thing."

CHAPTER SEVEN

Independent Promotion

I ndependent record promotion can be a challenging and demanding career for an outgoing individual with an interest in music and a talent for persuasion. The independent promoter is hired by record labels to persuade radio programmers to add a record to their station's playlist. Independent promoters work to get the "add" through phone calls, faxes, letters, and even taking the programmer out to dinner—anything they can do to persuade the programmer that the record they are "working" is a hit and worthy of being added to the station's playlist. One may ask, "If a record company has its own record promoters and promotion departments, why would it need to hire an independent promoter?" Often major labels want to be as thorough and aggressive as possible in their promotion tactics and, though they may have a national promotion director and a local promotion manager already calling a radio station, a third party—the independent promoter—only serves to put further pressure on that radio station to add a particular record. The thought is, the more people calling, the better, and if one record company uses independent promoters, then they all have to because one company does not want the competition to have any advantage that it doesn't enjoy.

A few years back, several scandals involving payola (paying radio stations to play records) rocked the independent promotion field and, for a time, lessened the influence of independents in the industry. These scandals are documented in the popular music business exposé *Hit Men* by Fredrick Dannen. Independent promotion, though, has rebounded from those troubled times and today enjoys as great an influence in the industry as ever. In most cases, independent promotion represents a step forward for those promotion people who work for major labels. It can be likened to going into business for yourself or striking out on your own. After gaining sufficient experience in the field of promotion at a record label, you may feel prepared to cut the cord and go into independent promotion.

Many independent promoters also come out of the field of radio. Many are former radio programmers who, for whatever reason, have left radio for the "other side." Independent promoters with radio backgrounds have a special advantage because of their experience being on the receiving end of other independent promoters' sales pitches. They know what approaches worked with them while they were in radio and which ones did not and can put this valuable insight into their own independent promotion work.

Whether you come into the field of independent promotion through the record industry or the radio industry, getting there and staying there depends primarily on one thing—relationships. It is the relationships with the radio and record people that you build over time that determine your effectiveness as a record promoter. If you are respected and well liked by many in the record industry, chances are a phone call from you will be a welcome and positive event rather than an annoyance. Often you can count on old friends to do a favor for you and add an important record for you at the right time. Promotion is a people business, and your success in this field depends greatly on your ability to interact positively with people.

An independent promoter can play an extremely important role for an independent record label. A small label with no promotion staff of its own may depend exclusively on the services of an independent promoter, with the independent promoter becoming the only contact between the label and radio stations. Thus, the independent promoter becomes more valuable and important in this scenario than to a major label.

Another type of independent promoter is the independent club promoter. Several promoters work exclusively with dance music and dance clubs. They call specific club deejays, usually those who report to the *Billboard* Dance Chart, in order to persuade them to add a particular record to their club playlists. This type of independent promotion requires the same persuasive talents that independent radio promotion requires—it is simply geared to a different group of people and a different kind of music. Both radio and club promotion on the independent level can be rewarding, depending on where your interest lies.

Bill Jerome, Independent Promoter

Veteran independent promoter Bill Jerome of Jerome Promotions and Marketing talks about the business of independent promotion.

Q: How did you break into the business of independent promotion?

"In the mid-seventies, I got a call from TK Records in Miami. KC and the Sunshine Band, who were on TK, wanted to hire me to do some promotion for them. I ended up doing independent promotion for their record 'Shake Your Booty.' TK Records liked what I did so they hired me full-time and I was there for seven years before they folded. I was there from beginning to end and one of the last people to go.

"I got the word when I was in Columbia, South Carolina, promoting KC. TK Records told me that they had to close up the shop. I didn't know what to do then, and I said to myself, 'I know everybody in the business, I know all the radio stations. Why not try it independently?' I did and it's gone well for eleven years now."

Q: Before independent promotion, you were a producer and you produced a few hits. What were they?

"One was 'Walk Away Renee' by The Left Bank and their follow-up 'Pretty Ballerina,' and 'Ding Dong the Witch is Dead' by the Fifth Estate. I also produced a hit that I am the artist on—an instrumental called 'Popcorn' by Hot Butter. And I had quite a few hits over in Europe with a girl group called Reparta."

Q: Why did you leave production for independent promotion?

"I had a record out with a record company that gave me some money to go on the road to promote it. I had so much fun that I really liked it. Producing is hard, and when you do get a hit record, you have to wait a long time to get paid. If you don't have a hit, you don't make that much money and then you've got to start taking money out of your own personal account to support yourself. I liked promotion a lot and it gave me steady money coming in. I do intend someday to go back into producing and, now that I know everybody in the promotion field and at the radio stations, my experience in independent promotion will make it easier for me to promote my own records when they come out."

Q: What skills and/or education does one need to make it in independent promotion?

"The best education is being out there on the street. You've got to be out there meeting the people, going to the radio stations. You see, with TK Records, I had to hit every radio antenna that I'd see along the way. They supplied me with a brand new car every year and what I did was I never called anybody to tell them I was coming. I just dropped in with a truck full of records. Sometimes I'd see an antenna on the side of the road and I would pull in and it would be a construction company! The best thing to do is get out there on the streets and get to know the people and, of course, it helps to know what's happening in the music business through the trade papers."

Q: Describe your job—what exactly do you do?

"Well, when somebody hires us to promote a new record, we call up stations all around the country, friends that we have, and find out if they received the record and if they're into it and can play it. Then if they can air the record, we work to get them to add it to their playlist and report it to the trades."

Q: What do you like most about your job?

"It's interesting. It's in the entertainment field and it's very exciting. What I love most is talking to a lot of nice people around the country. It's a big business, but it's small. Everybody knows everybody else and it's like a family. It's fabulous."

Q: What's the most challenging aspect of your job?

"The most challenging aspect is knowing that you have a hit record on your hands and you get these excuses from the radio station that they're going to "watch it" and see what happens; they don't want to go out on a limb and take a chance on it. You've just got to keep pounding them every week and inform them what's happening in other parts of the country."

Q: Do you think it's gotten tougher over the years?

"Oh, definitely. It was definitely easier in the TK Records days because there weren't 'plays per week,' there were only charts numbers, you know, from ten to nine to eight. And the charts were much bigger. They used to go from one to fifty. Now they go from one to thirty, one to twenty, and once in a while there's a station that goes one to forty. It is tougher now. There are more records out there now and all the stations want to go with the name acts.

"I also do promotion to the Gavin stations, the smaller market stations that report their playlists to *The Gavin Report*, but the major market stations are much tougher. It's much harder for them to go out on a limb for a new artist, a new record company. With the Gavin stations, you can go and get a feel on a record to see if there's anything there. You'll know in five to six weeks whether you have a record or not. Then you can bring it up to the second level and go to the major markets. It's much easier at the smaller markets because most of them will take a chance on a record."

Q: How does independent promotion differ from working as a promoter for a record label?

"In independent promotion, you can come and go as you please. There's no boss over you. You have a lot of pressure, don't get me wrong. But you don't have to go into these meaningless marketing meetings and phone conference calls with the whole world—all the branches across the country. To me that's a waste of time. I'd rather get on the phones and keep calling the stations. I definitely prefer to be independent."

Q: What advice would you give to someone who wants to get into independent promotion?

"The advice that I would give them is work hard, be honest, keep trying your best, and don't let anybody talk you out of it. If you feel that you can do it, just keep punching away."

CHAPTER EIGHT

Record Distribution

R ecord distribution forms the essential link between the record label and the consumer. The record label manufactures the records—although now it's almost exclusively CDs and cassettes—and the record distributor, in turn, sells the records to retail chains and independent record stores across the country. The record distributor has the network and staff to sell to the retail outlets and to do the necessary follow-up to make sure that the records are properly placed and selling. A good distributor can do wonders for a record with agressive promotion and marketing at the retail level. This can include point-of-purchase displays, local advertising, listening stations, or special placement. On a new release by a new artist, the distributor can play a key role in "breaking" that artist by convincing major chains and local record stores to stock and promote the record. Obviously, a record label itself can't do the job of the distributor—although several major labels have their own distribution arms (WEA, CEMA, BMG, UNI, Sony).

A national record distributor has sales representatives in key cities who visit retail accounts regularly to promote and sell that distributor's releases. It is this kind of ground-level promotion that sells records and proves the importance of the distributor. The sales representatives eventually develop personal relationships with their accounts, and this can be a big plus for the distributor. The record distributor can also coordinate national and regional advertising and listening station promotions with particular retail chains, which can have a big impact on sales. Interhit Records' first full-length release sold over

150,000 copies, mostly through well-placed and well-timed listening station promotions at major retail chains. Record distribution can be an exciting career for those who like to "work in the trenches," who enjoy sales and marketing, and who thrill at seeing a record "break big."

Fred Held, Distribution Promotion

Fred Held has spent thirty years in the music business—much of this time in independent distribution. Fred currently serves as national promotion director for MS Distributing Co.

Q: How did you break into the business?

"Back in 1966, I was an art major at the University of Miami. I went to visit a friend in a department store, turned in an application, and the next thing I knew they asked me if I could start tomorrow. I worked in the toy department through Christmas and then the day after Christmas they put me in the record department. Even though I liked music, I knew nothing about records. The day I started, the manager quit, so I quickly inherited that job. In six years of retail, I bought from about twenty different vendors, and I learned from my vendors and my customers about music and records. You'll hear this word quite often when you talk with me—*relationships*. It's a people business. Through my vendors, I learned what they could and could not get away with and, in turn, I used that when I went to wholesale.

"From '70 through '76 I worked for United Artists and Polydor. I started in sales and promotion, though primarily I worked in sales. Then from '76 through '87, I worked in independent distribution for different companies, including my own. I started my own company in '85 and left in '87 because— piece of advice—if you ever get in partnerships with your friends, make believe you're going in partnership with your enemies. Expect the worst and cover all the bases in front, so there's no surprises on the way out.

"After that I moved to Atlanta and stayed there from '87 through '91. I worked for two other distributors—very profitable—doing Southeast sales, promotion, buying, counseling, whatever. That's how I got the nickname Dr. Fred. Then in '91 I went to work for a new label named Cheetah Records out of Orlando, Florida. We got three gold albums and quite a bit of money. I left to start my own promotion and marketing company from '92 to '93. I did very well just on my name and the relationships that I had built up over the years. At the end of '93, one of the largest regional distributors—MS Distributing Co. based in Illinois, which I dealt with as a competitor, as a friend, and as a consultant—asked me to come on board as national promotion director and that's where I am today."

Q: How would you define record distribution for someone who knew nothing about it?

"Say John Smith and his family are starting a record company and they don't have the connections. They might have connections locally, but they don't have connections regionally or nationally. Well, they need to get with somebody who is established at retail, club, radio, wholesale, rackjobber entities around the region or around the country. Thus, they shop their product or their label to the distributors. Even if they have the budget, the connections, and the know-how, it would much more time consuming to do it on their own. So they get involved with a distributor, whether it be a branch operation at a major label like RCA or Capitol or Columbia or Warner Bros. or Atlantic or an independent distribution outfit, such as MS Distributing. As a vendor—a new label or an established label—dealing with your distributor, you must *think as your target*, whether it be a small chain of stores or a national chain of stores or a one-stop, which is one place that has about every product in the world because you can't buy direct from all these different vendors. For instance, let's take a radio station. What does that station need from you? Not what can you do for the station, but what does that station need from you? What does an account need from you? Think as your target and you'll get further. At a radio station, know your promotion director, your sales managers, your music directors, your program directors, and your mix-show jocks, if it's that genre of music. Know your receptionists—very important to know those receptionists. They're the first people who will get you in the door. Give them a couple of goodie promos. Remember birthdays. I repeat—people and relationships."

Q: What skills and/or education does one need to make it in record distribution?

"There are two qualifications you must have. It's very good to learn the basics of business in school, but there are two basics you must have: a brain and a hunger to learn the business. I'm still learning every day. You're going to fall down. You're going to make big mistakes. You take little steps at a time, and I repeat that people and the relationships you build with them are more important than the product."

Q: What exactly do you do?

"I am currently national promotion and marketing director. I deal with promotion and marketing at retail, wholesale, radio, and club levels. I deal with the sales managers and the vendors regarding realistic advertising and marketing proposals to build up the product and the vendor visibility on a regional and national basis. Because of my varied background I don't have time obviously to hit every station and every format of music. So with the various vendors I represent I advise them on what I can do, what they should be doing regarding marketing, publicity, and realistic promotion and marketing at the account level, regional level, and wholesale level in conjunction with our sales managers. A vendor or record company must have three things. Number one is product, meaning product flow. If a record company does not have six to ten singles and full-lengths a year, it's not good business for a national distributor to deal with them because it's more paperwork and time comsuming than it's worth. Number two, they must have personnel—not the amount of personnel, but the type of personnel who are willing to learn and are willing to work with their distribution outlets and with the marketing people and the contractors they hire on the outside. Number three, they must have a realistic budget to deal with the first hit. It's a major disaster if the first release you have is a hit and you can't afford it! On the other hand, maybe the first three records are worth nothing and you've spent all the money and you're getting nowhere. You must be very realistic. I have an expression, 'Friends and egos do not pay bills.' Listen to strangers. Listen to people who have been around. They will not steer you wrong because both of you want to make profits. They're not going to tell you what you want to hear—they'll tell you the truth."

Q: *What does the sales manager or sales director do?*

"I open up a door and then the sales manager directs the regional reps or the national reps, depending on what area he or she covers. The sales manager will have the expertise—more so than myself—on changes in the marketplace and the territory: constant happenings at a retail and wholesale level, personnel changes, buyouts, whatever. The vendor and the distributor are in sync on a realistic level."

Q: *What do you like most about your job?*

"In November of '95, I started my thirtieth year in the record business, and 95 percent of the time I can say I had fun. It's business, bottom line, but you have to have fun. Enjoy what you do, whether you're selling shirts at Bloomingdales or working in the record business, or else you're not fulfilling yourself or the people you work with or for. I have fun doing it. I love helping people grow. It all comes around, whether you sell five hundred pieces or have a million seller. You are involved and watch it happen. The same people come around with a different company or the same company—it all comes around again and again and again."

Q: What's the most challenging aspect of your job?

"Dealing with the labels that don't have a clue. As I said earlier, they could have a lot of money and tons of power, but they won't do anything themselves and they tell you after the fact that they didn't. They're defeating you and themselves. I don't know everything. I'm learning every day, but I can tell in a three to five minutes of conversation about a new vendor if they know what they're talking about or they're just telling me what I want to hear. I don't want to babysit. I don't mind holding a hand going uphill, but I don't feel like babysitting if I'm dealing with idiots. I don't want to waste my time or their time. I have too many other people I represent who are trying to do it the right way and take the right steps."

Q: What advice would you give someone interested in record distribution?

"You might have to work for free or for some promo items or free tickets, but if you want to get into the business starting from the ground up, if you really care about the record industry—whether it be engineering, production, manufacturing, distribution, promotion, publicity, booking, or management—learn and take slow steps. But have fun doing it."

CHAPTER NINE

Retail

M any a record executive started out working for the
local record store. For many with a desire to break
into the music business, a job in music retail can be
a great education. You get to see firsthand what makes a record
sell, which records sell, what music consumers respond to at the
street level, what retail buying patterns exist, and so on. Working in music retail allows for contact with record distributors,
record labels, and even artists. Also, you hear the latest music
first! All-in-all, a job at a record store can be a valuable learning experience and great way for a young person to get a first
taste of the business.

Of course, for those who enjoy the retail side of the business,
there is always opportunity to climb the ladder to higher-level
jobs. A salesperson can become a store manager, and a store
manager can become a regional manager and so on. You might
find great satisfaction in owning your own independent retail
store and enjoying the benefits of being your own boss and
doing something that you love. A wide variety of career opportunities can be found working for the many music retail chains
across the country. Well-known chains like Blockbuster Music,
Tower Records, Musicland, Wherehouse, Transworld, The
Wall, and others offer opportunity for advancement within the
corporate structure. As in any company, one can rise from store
clerk to top-level management in music retail with the right
amount of desire, dedication, and hard work. On the other
hand, the experience you gain working in music retail can pre-
pare for a career in record distribution, sales and marketing for

a record label, and other related industry fields. The contacts you make while interacting with distributors and record labels may one day lead to an unexpected job offer in the music industry outside of retail. Music retail can be a fast-paced, busy, demanding career, but if you love the business and love to sell, this may be your cup of tea."

Diane Bizier, Sales Representative

A music retail veteran who has worked in several different areas of retail in several different capacities is Diane Bizier. Diane's current position is that of Southeast Sales Representative for MS Distributing Co. She takes us inside the world of music retail.

Q: How did you break into music retail?

"I'd always been involved in music in one way or another, whether it be performing in a band or being a deejay. Through my connections, I knew someone that ran a record store and after college I became a sales clerk. I started at the very bottom.

"From sales clerk I was promoted to assistant manager at the same store. And a few months later, through a lot of hard work, I ended up running my own store for a fairly large chain. I ran one store for them and then they decided to give me another higher-volume store. So I ran two stores for this one company. Then I was recruited by another chain of stores to work for them. I became a manager-in-training, obviously, because it was a different company. I was a manager-in-training at one location and then ended up running two stores for the new chain. I ended up getting promoted to inventory audit supervisor, where I would travel throughout the chain, handling the inventories, checking product, and making sure the correct product was in the correct store. I was basically a troubleshooter. That job also led to a promotion where I was made the director of audio for a sister company, a chain of video stores that decided to add music departments. I was in charge of all the music departments. I had sixty-one stores underneath me. So that was fun.

"At that point, due to restructuring in the company, I was made a regional marketing manager. In order to further my involvement in the music industry, I took a job as a director of advertising for a chain of ten stores. It was a different aspect of the music business—the advertising part of it—so I decided to start small, with a ten-store chain. That was my last retail job. At retail, I feel I've done it all."

Q: What education does one need to make it in music retail?

"I have a minor in marketing. My degree, believe it or not, is in biology. I think just the fact that you have a four-year degree shows a prospective employer in any field that you have goals, you set goals, you achieve goals, and you are able to do the four years, which is very tough. College is fun, but it's tough. Any skills you learn in college can be applied to the music business. A lot of discipline went into being away from home, making myself go to classes every day, even though I didn't want to. Even if your degree isn't in the music business or in business, I found having done the four years very helpful to me in the long run in getting promoted."

Q: What skills does one need to be effective in a retail environment?

"Organization, obviously people skills, math skills—for closing out the books at the end of the night, you definitely have to have math skills. A lot of times it's common sense, too. Psychology can't hurt because, if you're a store manager, you do have people working under you and—believe it or not—some will come in and you will hear a lot of their problems, which will affect your store, such as people calling in because something personal's happened. A lot of times, these are younger people. Once you become a manager, you have to deal with this. Sometimes you need to have a good ear for your employee relations."

Q: As a store manager, what were your duties?

"Scheduling, making sure that the store is covered at all hours, that you don't have only one person on the floor, counting down the drawers, making sure the money that was made during the day matches up with the register tapes, which can get pretty crazy sometimes. Training new employees, overseeing employees, delegating responsibilities, and making sure those responsibilities get done. Ordering product either from a one-stop or going through the corporate channels necessary to get what my particular store needs. Mopping floors, alphabetizing, checking in shipments. A manager has to do everything."

Q: Did you listen to a lot of music to decide whether it would sell?

"Oh yes. I used to call it playing deejay. Customer service—suggestive selling—is a big thing. You find out what customers like and then expand from there. Show them some other types of music they might consider, but to do that you have to be very well versed in music. You learn to listen to everything and be open minded. Don't say, 'Oh, I only like country,' or 'I only like rock.' There's good and bad music in every genre, and that's very important to keep in mind."

Q: What do you like most about working in retail?

"The people and the music. The people are there because they have the same love you do—music. It's my passion, so it's not even a job to me. I have a good time when I do it. I can sit there and talk to people and make people happy. If you turn them on to something really good, it's nice to see a smile on their face, especially when customers come back and say, 'Hey I really liked what you suggested.' It makes you feel good."

Q: What is the most challenging aspect of the job?

"A lot of long hours. Rock and roll just doesn't sleep. It goes on and on and on. Some days can be long, but they're rewarding. I think that was the toughest part. Sometimes I'd rather be out partying with my friends, but I worked."

Q: What advice would you give to someone who wants a career in music retail?

"Get your foot in the door. Start setting your goals early. I knew that even though I did have a college degree, I wasn't going to go immediately into a management position or anything higher. I had to start as a sales clerk. Granted, I didn't make a lot of money, but in the long run it paid off. So once I achieved one goal, such as being a sales clerk, then I said, 'Okay, I'm going to try for assistant manager,' and I just slowly moved up. Just set goals for yourself and go for it."

CHAPTER TEN

Music Publishing

Music publishing can be a fascinating field for those interested in promoting the song itself. The music publisher takes care of the business of promotion, exploitation, and administration of songs. The publisher finds artists to record the song, issues licenses, collects the money, and pays the writer. Traditionally, when a publisher makes a deal with a songwriter, he or she takes on these obligations along with all rights to the song's copyright and 50 percent of the song's income. Often a songwriter doesn't have the contacts and the business savvy to handle the exploitation of a song and many times doesn't want to be concerned with the business side. The publisher, through his or her contacts, may be able to get the song to a major artist and thus create income that the songwriter most likely wouldn't be able to create alone. This is how the music publisher earns that 50 percent. After all, for the struggling songwriter, 50 percent of something is better than 100 percent of nothing. This is why many songwriters sign publishing contracts early in their careers. After they are established, they may decide to renegotiate a better deal or publish their songs themselves.

In the early days before the Rock Era, most artists didn't write their own songs and, therefore, publishers were arguably the most powerful people in the music business. Because no one can record a song without the publisher's permission, publishers could decide which artist would get to record the hottest new songs. Also, because of the power they wielded, it became nearly impossible for songwriters to sell their songs without a major publisher behind them. Today, many artists write and publish their own songs, so the need for a publisher to bring them songs to record has diminished. Many of the big songwriters today publish their own songs because their stature brings the big artists directly to them when they need that 'hit' song. Though music publishers aren't as powerful as they were in the old days, they still play a major role in the business today. Though many of the larger publishing companies merely act as administrators, there are publishers, large and small, who actively sign new writers, help them fine-tune their craft, put them together with other writers and artists, and guide their careers. Some publishers seek out new bands and artists to sign before they are signed to a record deal and, after working with them, actually help them to land record deals.

A song can generate two main sources of income. The first is mechanical royalties, which are paid by the record company to the publisher for each record sold. The rate is fixed and is usually paid quarterly. The publisher, after receiving the mechanical royalties, then divides them with the songwriter. The second source of song income is performance royalties, which are paid to the publisher by performance rights societies such as BMI, ASCAP, and SESAC. These royalties are based on public performances of the song on radio, on TV, in movies, in nightclubs, or in concerts. Like mechanical royalties, performance royalties are paid based on a fixed rate per play. This rate increases with the number of performances the song receives. Obviously, the return on a hit record can be enormous. This is why music publishing can be a lucrative field for both the publisher and the songwriter.

There are many different opportunities in the world of music publishing. A publishing company can be a international corporation or a one-person operation. If you love music, enjoy working with creative people, and have a flair for the business side, music publishing may be your arena. If you are a songwriter, you may want to consider being your own publisher.

For more information on setting up your own publishing company, you can contact one of the following performing rights societies:

BMI
320 West 57th Street
New York, NY 10019

ASCAP
One Lincoln Plaza
New York, NY 10023

SESAC
421 West 54th Street
New York, NY 10019

Randy Poe, Music Publisher

A music publishing executive with a world of experience in the field, Randy Poe, executive vice-president and general manager of Leiber and Stoller Music, oversees the catalog of songwriting legends Jerry Leiber and Mike Stoller, which includes such rock classics as "Hound Dog," "Jailhouse Rock," "Kansas City," and countless others. Randy has also written a successful book on music publishing titled *Music Publishing: A Songwriter's Guide*, which won the coveted ASCAP Deems Taylor Award. In the following interview, Randy shares his wealth of knowledge on music publishing.

Q: How did you break into music publishing?

"I came at it sideways. When I was in college, I took some courses on the music business, including one on how a record company works and one on how a publishing company works.

That was helpful for me, but I really started in radio. I was based out of Muscle Scholls, Alabama, which throughout the sixties and seventies had a huge recording industry. Everybody was cutting albums down there. It started as a soul thing with Aretha Franklin and Percy Sledge and Wilson Pickett and those guys. Then, in the seventies, The Rolling Stones and Linda Ronstadt and Joe Cocker all came down. Eventually it turned into more of a place for country writers to get away from Nashville. Shenandoah and folks like that were cutting down there in the eighties. At the end of the seventies, I moved to New York. Actually, it was kind of a 'wing and a prayer' situation because I only had a couple of suitcases and moved there on a Greyhound bus using the logic that if eight million people could survive, so could I. And I learned that if you can type, you can survive in New York City. I guess that today it probably would be if you know how to work a word processor, then you can survive. I went to work temping at different music publishing companies because that's where I wanted to get my foot in the door. One of those, an old time print publisher named Carl Fischer, hired me.

"I eventually left there and went to work for an organization called the Songwriter's Hall of Fame in New York. That's where everything fell together for me because over the course of the three or four years that I was there, I got to meet everybody in the music business and a lot people in the entertainment business in general. Not to drop names, but I actually got to spend time with people like Bob Dylan, Willie Nelson, and Dick Clark and songwriters like Leiber and Stoller, Mann and Weil, Carole King, Gerry Goffin, Sammy Cahn, Jules Stein, and a lot of the great songwriters from the forties, fifties, and sixties. Luckily, I was befriended by Leiber and Stoller and, since I already knew something about music publishing from the class I had taken and from the fact that I had already been in publishing a little bit in New York, they brought me on board in 1985. It was a one-room, one-person office in New York. We now have over a dozen people on staff and a fully functioning publishing company here in Los Angeles."

Q: So what skills and/or education does one need to make it in music publishing?

"It really depends on which area of music publishing you're going to get into. For instance, one of the important areas of music publishing is the handling of the royalties coming in and going out. So probably you would need to have a degree in accounting to be able to even think about working in that particular area of the industry. As far as the licensing end, you just have to be a good negotiator. The key skill to me in music publishing and maybe in the music business in general is the whole negotiation process. It's also possibly the most entertaining part. There is not a day that goes by that we don't get asked to have one of our songs used either in a motion picture or a television show or in a commercial or some other use of some type. We have to figure out the value of this particular song in this particular situation and then we have to convince the user that that's the right amount. It really is a negotiation process. It's almost like politics—you really have to be good at that aspect of the business to survive.

"Depending on the size of your catalog, you can make millions. I've seen it happen. I've seen one song over the course of three or four years gross over a million dollars because of one commercial. In negotiating, you have to be able to feel out the other party to see how far they are willing to go with a price. I know it's not something that people usually think about in the music business, but it really is dollars and cents in a lot of ways. So it's best to make as many dollars and cents as you can in that particular area and that's what the licensing person does.

"As far as the copyright end of things, business affairs and copyright go hand in hand. That's something you learn by doing. Obviously, if you're a paralegal, you would probably be able to get into that door a lot easier than somebody just coming in off the street. A lot of publishing companies today actually hire lawyers to handle their business affairs department. That's good, too, but I've certainly known a lot of people who can handle copyright and business affairs without having a law degree.

"To succeed in the creative end you need to have good ears and also a lot of contacts in the business. Our main thrust with the kind of catalog that we have—hits from the fifties, sixties, and seventies—is mainly to get those songs into film and television because people tend to want to use songs that have a nostalgic feel to them, that everybody recognizes, as opposed to using material that's on the charts right this second. So I hired somebody who had a lot of contacts in the film and TV world in Hollywood and though he didn't necessarily know the catalog the day he walked into the door, he certainly does now. He's more of a street person, somebody who can get out there and pitch anything to anybody. So if you're a good salesperson, that's really what the creative person is doing: selling the product."

Q: Describe your job. What exactly do you do?

"There was a time when I did everything I just described—all at once. That's why I have very little hair on top of my head. Now I oversee the entire company, which is thirty-five thousand copyrights as well as the production company. Leiber and Stoller themselves didn't write those thirty-five thousand songs, but they wrote about four hundred of them. We have a catalog of songs going all the way back to the thirties—although most of them are hits from the fifties, sixties, and seventies. I've done a little bit of everything. I pitch tunes. I oversee all of the other people who are involved in the company. When I go in in the morning, I never know exactly what's going to happen. Every night before I go home, I make a list of the four or five things I'm going to attempt to accomplish the next day. But usually when I walk in the door, there are already people walking into my office asking me questions, telling me what's going on and asking me how much should we charge for this, saying, 'Here's the theme for the film. Have you got a good idea for what song would fit?' and asking me about lawsuits that are going on. Anytime you have a company with thirty-five thousand songs, there are lawsuits going every direction. I remember years ago seeing John Lennon talking about being involved into the last decade of his life with lawsuits and not really wanting to continue every day to end up in another lawsuit with somebody. At the time I heard him say that, I thought, 'Well that's really sad.' And looking back now, I've been involved in lawsuits every day of my life for the last eleven years. Usually it's things like copyright infringement. We had several cases that were settled out of court so they don't really end up getting to be publicly known. We have situations where we have songs that should revert back to us at the end of the second term of copyright and we have to go after them aggressively. We have people who claim songs that are ours and we have to stop them. So for me a little bit of every day is involved in one lawsuit or another and that's the least fun part of the job.

"I work at acquiring catalogs, keeping my nose to the ground to find out what's out there, doing in administration deals with various people. For example, a royalty person will come into my office and say, 'Here's a title of the song in French, what do you think it would be in English because I can't find anything that tells me what song this is.' I mean, there's just all sorts of goofball things that go on all day long. In my particular case, I've got both Jerry Leiber and Mike Stoller, the two owners of the company, asking me questions, wanting to know what's going on. So it's a chain that always seems to end up at my desk. I'm mainly the guy responsible for somehow making the business continue to function everyday."

Q: *What do you like most about the job?*

"For me it's a lot of fun when somebody uses a tune that was your idea. I think the creative end is probably the most fun for anybody. *Home Improvement* a few weeks ago was wanting to use a song they couldn't get and they came to us at the last second saying, 'Fit something in this spot, and it has to be funny. Can you do it and clear it today? And come up with numbers today? And let's have the deal done by tonight.' To be able to come up with the song, to be able to come up with a punch line for the script that works with the song and be able to actually get my licensing person to negotiate numbers in a matter of minutes with the clearance person at *Home Improvement* was a great thing. It was really fun. Then to watch it on TV about a month later and see it all unfold was really great.

"Getting tunes cut by the big artists is also fun. Another really fun part of my job is reissues. Over the course of the last five or six years, I've gotten very heavily involved in reissues. We've taken parts of the catalog and done some really fun things. With Rhino Records we did a thing called *There's a Riot Going On: Eighteen Rock 'n Roll Classics of Leiber and Stoller*, which includes two Elvis cuts. It was the very first time RCA allowed somebody besides RCA to put out Elvis tracks. We did a thing called *Fifty Coastin' Classics*, a two-CD anthology of the Coasters, which was really fun. Then we did a single CD, *Very Best of the Coasters*, with Rhino. I did a thing with K-TEL called *The Best of Kansas City*, which was ten different versions of the song 'Kansas City.' It was Jerry's idea. Jerry told me years ago, 'You know what you can do? You can put together a tape and have all the different versions of Kansas City on it, and you can sell it.' And I said 'Well, who would buy it?' But it turned out that after *The Best of Louie, Louie* came out on Rhino and sold really well, we sat down and came up with ten diverse-enough versions of 'Kansas City' that the listener wouldn't go crazy, and we sequenced it in such a way that you don't really think about it being the same song ten times in a row. It's ten completely different versions of the same song.

"That's been a real fun part of the job because it's something tangible. So much of what you do when you're in music publishing is really not tangible. I think that's why people who want to use songs find it so difficult to understand why it costs so much money—and it does cost a lot of money—because it's this seemingly free-floating thing in the air. So when you're working in that kind of a service business, you don't generally get to see any kind of tangible results. The checks go by your desk, but other than that it's just gone.

"I've also done a lot of fun things that probably don't mean a lot to society at large. When we first started doing our print division with Warner Bros., we came up with some cool things such as 'Jailhouse Rock' sheet music that has a picture of Leiber and Stoller with Elvis in one corner and a scene from *Jailhouse Rock* in the other. Until that time—this was 1986, I believe—there had never been an Elvis sheet music with anybody else on the cover but Elvis. We kind of like to do little things that maybe only three or four of us realize is cool, but it's still fun to do."

Q: What's the most challenging aspect of the job?

"I think whenever you get more than one person in a room it's always a challenge. I'm not the best in the world at handling personnel crises, and that sort of thing is inevitable. If you're a one-person operation, you don't have anybody that you can blame for anything going wrong but yourself. If you're a three-person operation, then you have at least three people you can blame, and at least three of them don't want to take the blame! So that end of it is not a lot of fun for me because I prefer to be doing the creative thing and the negotiating end of it. My least favorite part would be telling this person to get off that person's back.

"As far as the most challenging part, the same things that are the most fun are also the most challenging. When I first decided that reissues would be a good way to go, it was really difficult to get anybody to understand why people would want to buy a record of songs by two songwriters who were really relatively unknown entities. I mean, maybe you know who Leiber and Stoller are and I've certainly stumbled across people who do, but they have never, ever been the kind of household names that a lot of other songwriters have been, and that's been intentional. They didn't want to be recognized on the street every five minutes. They didn't want to develop the kind of reputations that some other songwriters had. They simply wanted to live their lives, write songs, and live happily ever after. And I think they've done that, but luckily over the last few years they've begun to test the waters to see what it's like to let people know that they exist. I think the primary way that's taken place is through *Smokey Joe's Cafe: Songs of Leiber and Stoller*, which has been on Broadway for over a year and has sold 95 percent of capacity every single night for over a year. A little bit later this year, it will tour both England and Australia. I think it'll last on Broadway for years to come. Until that came out, the names Leiber and Stoller were not that well known. They didn't do that many interviews, they didn't like to do TV shows. So when I was going to Rhino and to RCA and to other labels saying 'Let's do something that's Leiber and Stoller-related,' they were saying, 'That's nice, but who's going to buy it?' The end result is we got RCA to put out something called *Elvis Presley Sings Leiber and Stoller*, which includes maybe twenty-one or twenty-two of the songs that they wrote for Elvis, including a number of hits. I think the results have been quite good. And then because of the Broadway show's success, people have gone out and picked up the Rhino CD, *There's a Riot Going On*, because many of the original versions of the songs from the show are on the *Riot* CD. That was a real challenge, to get people excited about doing these kind of compilations and reissues. To this day, there are other things that I'm still trying to get released and reissued and have not been able to. Eventually I will, but it's a real challenge because I know they will sell and it's incomprehensible to me that other people at record labels don't understand that.

"The other part that's a challenge, which is a good challenge, is the whole negotiating process. For example, usually when you're quoting for a motion picture, you're quoting what's called a flat fee with a video buyout. In 1996, it's not realistic anymore to think that you're going to be able to charge a fee for every video sold. What's happened is that the whole industry has gone to a video buyout option. I can't really talk about numbers because the numbers can be anything. For a little short use with a not very well-known song, you could be talking about $7,500 to $10,000—next to nothing in music publishing terms. But for a big song over opening credits or over the closing credits or over the title of the movie, we can be talking well over $100,000. From time to time people come to you with small pictures, and the real challenge is to find a way to let them use the song if you think it's a good use and you know they've got no money. So on occasion we've said 'Alright, we'll schedule this, we'll come up with a situation where you can use the song for next to nothing. And then if your movie makes it to the million-dollar range, then you'll have to pay us an additional fee because we know you'll be making a profit by then.' We had one film where they said, 'We can't do that, but we'll pay a royalty on the video.' It was just a rare opportunity to get a royalty on a video, so we said okay, ten cents a video. For them it didn't really matter. If the video ever comes out, it'll be great. They said, 'You'll get your ten cents a video, if we can even find a distributor.' I won't say what the movie is, but I'll tell you that the other day we got a check for $257,000, and the ultimate irony is that this was a situation where it makes no sense because huge, major motion pictures come out every day and all these huge, major motion picture people say we can't afford to pay you a royalty on the video and the most we can possibly pay you for, to use your song on this film, is $25,000. And here is a small movie that ended up doing great in the home video market and, even though it's only been out a few weeks, it's already grossed us over a quarter of a million dollars. It started out as a challenge just trying to find a way to be able to let these people to use this song for their little film and the end result was it paid off."

Q: What advice would you give someone who wants to get into music publishing?

"There are a lot of different ways you can go. The number-one piece of advice that I was given, and I would never have thought of this on my own, as simple and logical and obvious as it is, was 'It's not what you know, it's who you know.' I really took that to heart. When I moved to New York, I didn't know anybody. I'm not just talking about the music business—I didn't know *anybody*. And somehow I managed to find a way to start meeting the people I needed to know to get my foot in the door. Of course, not every person can move to New York and stumble across a job where they're meeting Bob Dylan inside of a year. I realize that's not a realistic statement, but what you have to do is hang out with those who do know the people. There are all sorts of organizations—in Nashville, in New York, in Los Angeles—that cater to people in the business of songwriting, and these usually lead to people in the business of publishing. There are a couple of organizations out here in Los Angeles. The Association of Independent Music Publishers meets once a month at lunchtime and all sorts of important issues in the music publishing world get discussed. I have seen some of the most important people in the music publishing business there and have met some of them there. It's one of those places where you can go and pay for a typical hotel restaurant meal and you can, if you're aggressive enough, meet some important players

in the business. The same holds true for an organization called
The California Copyright Conference, which meets one night
a month at the Sportsman Lodge over in the Valley. It's more
of the same. Get involved with those organizations so you can
meet a lot of the people who are in the middle of the whole
music publishing business. Generally the other things that I
know about are more songwriter related. Songwriters Guild of
America has offices in New York, Los Angeles, and Nashville.
New York, of course, is where the National Music Publishers
Association itself is located—obviously not a bad bunch to be
involved with."

CHAPTER ELEVEN

Radio

R adio plays a vital role in the success of a record. Airplay on a radio station can mean increased visibility for the artist and increased sales in the marketplace. A radio hit can turn an album that has sold fifty thousand units into a million seller, and this phenomenon happens regularly. A recent example is the Warner Bros. Records act The Goo Goo Dolls, whose album *A Boy Named Goo* struggled early to sell twenty to thirty thousand units until Top-40, alternative, rock, and adult contemporary stations began playing the single "Name." The incredible public reaction to "Name" sent album sales over a million in a matter of months, and The Goo Goo Dolls went from being a cult favorite to a national pop success story. The power of radio cannot be underestimated when it comes to selling records. This is the reason that record companies sink so much money into promoting their records to the radio—the payoff is enormous. A career in radio can put you in the middle of the exciting process of breaking the hits of tomorrow.

Radio offers a variety of job opportunities for those willing to take the plunge. If you enjoy performing, but not on stage, a career as a radio deejay may be for you. To succeed as a deejay, you need to have a talent for public speaking, a good knowledge of music, a love of performance, and a thick skin. Many want to become radio deejays, but the jobs are scarce and the job security even scarcer. A career in radio is sure to include a lot of moving from place to place and an unfortunate tendency for termination. Due to the temporary nature of the radio business—the fact that stations change format, ownership, or management constantly—the turnover is great. So, be ready to be fired! Just remember that it's part of the business.

A step up from the radio deejay are the music director (MD) and the program director (PD). The program director guides the sound, the image, the personnel, and the direction of the station. The PD is the boss. It takes someone with a talent for management and great ears to rise to the position of program director. The PD is usually in charge of picking the music for the station, including deciding what records to add to a station's playlist. The PD is the one the record promoters must convince to add their records. A lot of pressures come with this job, but the personal and career rewards can be great.

Stations in medium to large markets often have music directors. The music director is in charge of overseeing the new music that is submitted for consideration and also is concerned with various other duties pertaining to the sound of the station. Some music directors actually pick the music to be added to the playlist themselves. At those stations, the program director is concerned mostly with the management of the station and leaves the music decisions to the music director. Often a radio deejay can become a music director and eventually a program director. Many of today's successful major market program directors started out as deejays in smaller markets and worked their way up the ladder.

Jhani Kaye, Program Director

One such success story is Jhani Kaye, program director for KOST 103.5 FM in Los Angeles—one of the most influential and popular adult contemporary radio stations in the country. Jhani talks about job opportunities in the world of music radio.

Q: How did you break into radio?

"I was a sophomore in high school when the phone rang one Saturday morning. A girl I had met in the principal's office earlier that year said she was snowed in and couldn't make it to do a show at the local radio station where the high school had a fifteen-minute program. I asked her why she was asking me to fill in and she said, 'You're in drama, and you do this kind of thing, and I think you can do it.' I said, 'Well what is it I have to do?' She said, 'Go to my locker at school. I'll give you the combination. Inside you'll find a prepared script. It's only fifteen minutes long. All you do is read it. There'll be an engineer at the radio station. He'll introduce you, and that's it!' I begrudgingly went to her locker because I really didn't want to do this to begin with, and I picked up the script. I then drove to the radio station. Imagine my amazement when I discovered that she had only written five minutes of material for fifteen minutes. So here I am with my reputation hanging out there and ten minutes to fill not knowing anything about ad-libbing in an aural medium. Somehow I made it through the longest fifteen minutes of my life and left the station very embarrassed and with great humility. I remembered thinking, 'I never want to do radio again.' Well, Mr. Larry Shields, the general manager of the radio station, happened to be listening to all this and he apparently heard some talent and potential. He went to great lengths to find out who I was because, being only a substitute host, no one really was aware of me. It took a couple of weeks before he finally discovered me. He then offered me work. So that's basically how it all started. I actually never had to work in noncommercial radio as many students today do. I had the opportunity to enter the industry directly via commercial radio."

Q: What skills and/or education does one need to break into radio?

"No one has ever asked me if I ever finished the third grade! Education is not an issue. It's only an issue if you want to go into management, but if you want to play the role of talent and be on the air, it truly comes down to performance and has nothing to do with education (other than that you should be able to speak the language and be grammatically correct with your language). Prior to the late 1980s, you had to have a radio license, and that typically required some technical schooling, but the Federal Communications Commission has since deregulated the licensing of talent and now anyone can go on the air as long as they're a citizen."

Q: Would someone have to go to school to be an engineer at a radio station?

"It's a little difficult for me to answer your question since I'm not an engineer, but most engineers have received some technical education early in their careers, whether it be repairing television sets or working on computers before they become employed in radio."

Q: What exactly do you do?

"A program director is responsible for the overall sound and image of the station presented to the audience. There are literally thousands of details that a program director handles every week. A few of the major ones include the hiring and termination of air talent, overseeing the marketing of the radio station (including logo design, television commercials, billboards, bus benches, helping to design the direct mail, telemarketing, etc.), as well as selecting and scheduling the music for the radio station, developing the formats of the radio station, determining stop-set times and construction, as well as a myriad of other functions. It also includes the creating and conceptualizing of jingles and other production elements. It really involves putting all the systems in place and then insuring that the systems are being honored by listening to the station daily."

Q: What do you like most about your job?

"The fact that the work is unconventional—not traditional. I'm one of a unique set of managers in the world of a multi-million-dollar facility who can choose to go to work in jeans and a T-shirt or a suit. It really doesn't matter. I pretty much get to call my own hours, and that's a great benefit to this type of work. You get to work with great people in a people-based industry. As a program director, you get to offer a lot of instruction, and that feels good to a person like myself because I enjoy knowing that people who have worked for me in the past have gone on to become program directors themselves. I have always felt that one of my responsibilities as a program director was to teach and conduct a programming school, as it were."

Q: What did you like most about being a disc jockey?

"It's a thrill that not everyone in this life has the opportunity to experience. People in radio, television, and film all have a common thread: the thrill of knowing that people are listening, watching, or reviewing their performance—and enjoying it. So you feed off that much as an actor on stage receives immediate feedback from the audience. There is an 'electricity' and magic that just seems to happen."

Q: What's the most challenging aspect of your job as program director?

"Deregulation of the radio industry has created less opportunity for individuals to own radio stations. Only large companies own a great many radio stations, even in a single market, given the deregulation that occurred in 1996. It's a real shame because when you have one company overseeing many operations, typically there's a consolidation of jobs, of duties, and certainly of talent. Talent becomes squelched when this happens. Some of my best times in radio were when I worked for individual owners who encouraged creativity, new ideas, and became mentors for me and many others."

Q: What advice would you give to someone who wants to break into radio?

"The initial advice I would offer is do not major in the field in college. So many young people get into this business and discover that it really isn't what they had hoped it would be. They then have to make a tough decision about what to do with the remainder of their lives. Unless you've studied something else in school, you end up putting all your eggs in one basket. The future requires one to be skillfully diverse. Business would be a great major because you can apply that to practically any career. Anyone contemplating a position in radio should take a hard look at the industry prior to entering it. There are fewer than ten thousand radio stations in the United States. Considering that there are only six full-time air talents on average at any radio station in the country...well, you can do the math. If you get more specific in your career goals and want to be a CHR air talent, which used to be called Top-40, you've cut your opportunities down to probably twelve hundred radio stations. That's seventy-two hundred jobs and probably tens of thousands of people attempting to fill them. So you have to realize that radio and television are very much like the railroads. The railroads were displaced by the airlines because trains could only go where tracks existed. The finite number of radio stations in the country liken radio to the railroads. This limits the opportunities.

"Perhaps the best advice I could give to a young person who wants to be an air talent in the industry is to be realistic about the salaries. They are never as high as you might have been led to believe. Also, you had better be ready to move a lot in this industry because to improve your career requires picking up stakes and relocating to another city. Therefore, it may behoove you to remain single because a husband or wife may have his or her own career goals (and may not be willing to pick up and leave as quickly as a disc jockey!) So, set realistic goals. One in fifty thousand people start in Los Angeles, Chicago, or New York. You are more than likely going to end up beginning a radio career in a Jackson, Mississippi, or a Barstow, California, and move from small markets to medium markets and then, if luck is with you and you possess the talent, you might have the opportunity to rise to the major markets and to all the glory and success that you dream of when you first enter the business.

CHAPTER TWELVE

Artist

Almost every singer and musician has dreamed of being "the star"—the one on stage—adored by millions. Well, it doesn't happen every day. Not everyone who picks up a guitar becomes the next Bruce Springsteen. If you have a burning desire to perform your own music, to entertain, to be the center of attention, to express yourself through music—you're probably already pursuing a career as an artist. Usually, it takes years of practice, performing, working, ups, downs, and even sideways before one succeeds in the music business as an artist. Sometimes someone is so gifted it practically happens overnight, but this is the exception to the rule. Usually success requires effort, so be ready to give all you've got. Perfect your craft—whether it be singing or playing an instrument. Don't give up. Believe in yourself. And don't let anyone tell you that you can't make it because anything is possible.

To give aspiring artists out there some insight into the world of those artists who have already made it, here are four superstar interviews I conducted on behalf of *DMA* magazine— Mariah Carey, Gloria Estefan, Donna Summer, and Ulf Ekberg of Ace of Base. All four of these world-famous artists have sold millions of records, and everyone who is working on a career in the music business as an artist can learn from their experiences.

Artist Profile: Mariah Carey

What more can be said about Mariah Carey? The biggest-selling female artist of the 1990s returns with her fifth album *Daydream* (Columbia)—the latest in an unbroken string of chart-topping and critically acclaimed albums and singles. Since her eponymous debut LP *Mariah Carey* in 1990, Mariah has sold over sixty million records worldwide—a third of these sales in the last twenty-four months. *Mariah Carey* sold over twelve million albums worldwide and yielded a record-setting four consecutive number-one singles—"Vision of Love," "Love Takes Time," "Someday," and "I Don't Wanna Cry." The success of her first album also brought her two Grammy awards. *Emotions* (1992) and *MTV Unplugged* (1992) brought millions more in sales and several more hit singles. Then, in 1993 Mariah released *Music Box*, which—propelled by the massive hits "Dreamlover" and "Hero"—sold more than twenty-four million copies worldwide! Even last year's holiday album— *Merry Christmas*—resulted in over eight million in sales. Mariah's popularity, as well as her sales figures, are truly staggering. The one-time coat check girl has certainly made it to the big time in a big way. "Sometimes I have to stop and reflect on all that's happened to me," says Mariah. "I'm really living a dream because this is what I wanted to do throughout my entire life."

Daydream finds Mariah more mature, more restrained, and more creative than ever. Produced by Mariah and Walter Afanasieff with individual tracks produced by David Morales and Mariah ("Daydream Interlude" [Fantasy Sweet Dub Mix]"); Dave Hall and Mariah ("Fantasy"); and Jermaine Dupri, Manuel Seal, and Mariah ("Always Be My Baby," "Long Ago"), all of the songs on *Daydream*, with the exception of her cover version of Journey's "Open Arms," were written or cowritten by Mariah Carey. Two of the highlights on the album are the special guest appearances of Boyz II Men on "One Sweet Day" and Babyface on "Melt Away." Collaboration forms an important part of Mariah's creative process. "When I work with someone, no matter who it is, it still has to have my sound on it. It can't be like I totally conform to somebody else's vibe and sound and negate what my own sound is. I like to work with people who are more street in terms of the music they make, then I put my thing on top of theirs. It gives me the most pleasure to interact with new people in writing songs. It helps me to grow."

Daydream is Mariah's most R&B-oriented record to date. "I grew up on R&B music and I'm also a big fan of rap and hip-hop," says the artist. "When I began putting this album together, in addition to the more pop-oriented songs for which I've received much-appreciated support over the years, I also knew I wanted to explore more of my urban music roots this time." "Fantasy" provides a perfect example the R&B edge that permeates *Daydream*. The simultaneously released remix single produced by Sean "Puffy" Combs (Notorious B.I.G., May J. Blige, Jodeci) brings together Mariah and Wu Tang Clan for what may be the oddest pairing in recent memory. This remix proved an instant smash on The Box, BET, and other major urban radio stations. "Fantasy" entered both the Pop and R&B Charts at number one—a first-ever for any female artist. "I love the song because it covers so many bases and it gave me the opportunity to spread my wings beyond just singing," notes Mariah, who makes her directorial debut with the video for "Fantasy," filmed at Rye Playland, a vintage New York amusement park. "Before I mainly took direction, often thinking to myself that my videos could be better and much more reflective of the real me. When I felt I had experience and confidence to write and direct my own clips, I decided to go for it. It's difficult wearing all those hats, but the challenge and positive results are worth it. That's also why I plan to direct the rest of the *Daydream* videos. If they work, I'll take the credit. If they don't, I can handle the heat." Mariah Carey is constantly proving that her talents extend far beyond singing.

Regarding her unbelievable commercial success, Mariah remarks: "Of course, I'd be lying to say that I don't care about having to be successful. But I can't get wrapped up in that who insanity of, 'Oh, I have to beat myself this time' or 'I have to go to the next level.' I think when people start to be obsessed with that, it's the beginning of the end, really. Obviously, my surroundings have changed and the people around me have changed and the way that people I don't know react to me has changed. But I'm still the same person. I just have to be more careful in a lot of ways and more guarded."

At 25, she is still maturing as a performer and still as ambitious as ever. "I've always been 100 percent driven to do this," she says of her stardom. "Every minute of my life." One of the things that inspires her, she says, is "never wanting to have that feeling again of instability and that the rug could be pulled out from under me because that's how I always felt. I'm at a place where I'm more comfortable now—and I feel that it shows in the music. I try not to take anything for granted. I walk around the house and I look at things and I just remember what it was like not so long ago. I think that there will always be that person who didn't have enough growing up and who had this huge desire to have a career, to have any career in music, really. I'm very fortunate."

Her success allows her to give back to the community in many ways. Her commitment to the urban community can be seen in her successful "Camp Mariah" project, which is set up through New York's Fresh Air Fund. This camp gives disadvantaged inner-city kids a chance to go to summer camp. Committing $1 million to the project herself, she has already raised an additional $650,000 with a benefit concert held last December at New York's Cathedral of St. John the Divine.

Success, as is always the case, tends to bring one's personal life into the spotlight. Mariah Carey is no exception. She often complains that the press seems "obsessed" with her racial identity. "I view myself as a human being. My father's Venezuelan and black and my mother's Irish, and I consider myself to be a combination of all those things. To say I'm only one or the other would be negating the other things that I am." Also, questions of her relationship with her boss, Tommy Mottola, president of Sony Music Entertainment, have dogged her throughout her career. They married in 1993 and live in a beautiful and spacious mansion in New York's suburban Westchester County. Her success should have silenced the critics long ago who complained of "special treatment" because of her relationship with Mottola. "As far as music goes, we're pretty much in sync," reveals Mariah. "We have a great relationship and like anyone, we have to work things through."

Most recently, the press focused on the fact that Mariah's sister is HIV positive and that, according to some reports, Mariah's mother had taken her sister's son away from her. Says Mariah of her sister's troubles: "I haven't spoken to her in a long time, but I hope she's well. People don't realize we're all human beings and when they take your personal nightmares and make them public ones, it's very difficult. But everything seems to have worked itself out."

Another criticism that she has had to endure is the perceived overuse of her upper register. "I have to let the criticisms shake off of me," she says. "But on the new album, I tried to be more selective with where I placed my higher register. I tried to use it more as a texture rather than coming right out with the in-your-face thing. I think at times in the past I have gotten carried away with it because it's something I enjoy and it's a very freeing feeling. But on the new album I tried to tone it down and just use it in a more creative way, as a background part."

The club community has always played a big role in Mariah Carey's success, and her loyalty to the club community is reflected in the brilliant remixes and dance-oriented material that she has released over the years. Larry Flick, dance music/single reviews editor at *Billboard*, describes her as "the pop dynamo [who] never turns her back on the children of clubland who have long worshipped and supported her."

"Carey's ongoing commitment to dance music is especially laudable," he continues, "given how many of our homegrown divas abandon us once the mainstream world beckons. If there is one thing people in dance music love, it's a diva with a big, gorgeous voice. Certainly, Mariah has that and then some. There's also something to be said for the quality and tone of her material, which is generally uplifting and optimistic. Mariah is also larger than life—both in terms of her image and lifestyle. That's real attractive to people in clubs and very much in keeping with their patterns of embracing divas with whom we can vicariously entrust our fantasies."

The artist's club sensibilities especially shine through on "Fantasy" which, though permeated by an upbeat and thoroughly nineties sound, pays tribute to the eighties club sound with its inspired use of a sample from the Tom Tom Club's hit "Genius of Love." Mariah teams up with David Morales for the club mix of "Fantasy," which sports a deep house groove. "I've always enjoyed the process of going back and rethinking my songs in that context," says Mariah. "And David is just incredible to work with."

Erik Bradley, music director at B96 in Chicago, has nothing but praise for Mariah and David Morales: "Mariah Carey's music covers almost every base when it comes to pop culture. The David Morales remixes of 'Dreamlover' and 'Fantasy' have to go down as two of the most incredible reworkings ever. In my opinion, she is the premiere artist today because of her amazing versatility and flawless vocal skills!"

The future certainly looks bright for Mariah Carey. She has already accomplished what many singers can only dream of accomplishing, and she certainly can expect even greater success in the years to come. At the time of this interview, the singer was planning a prime-time TV special to be taped at

Madison Square Garden and an arena tour by Christmas. "I'm looking forward to the whole touring experience again," she says. "I'm starting from a different place inside of myself this time. I'm more relaxed."

Once Mariah completes her promotion for *Daydream*, she plans to launch her own Sony-distributed label, which is still in the early stages of discussion. "I love the idea of working with other artists," Mariah enthuses. "I'm not only about writing songs for myself. I enjoy the process of writing and producing songs that fit voices that are different from mine. And I love collaborating with different people." In the end, it comes down to Mariah's commitment to her music and to her many fans. "I've come to realize more than ever that it's the fans who can make or break you," says Mariah. "For me they are priority and are kept in mind as far as the quality and substance that has to go into every song I record, every live show I do, and every video I do."

Reprinted with permission from DMA magazine, December 1995

Artist Profile: Gloria Estefan

Ever since "Dr. Beat" thrilled clubgoers around the world in 1984, Gloria Estefan and Miami Sound Machine have held a special place in the hearts of dance music fans. In this interview, Gloria specifically credits the club community with launching her career ten years ago—a career that includes three double-platinum albums, three platinum albums, five gold singles, ten Top-10 pop hits, and two number-one pop hits. Sold-out tours in recent years continue to prove her popularity around the world. Gloria Estefan's new album *Hold Me, Thrill Me, Kiss Me* (Epic) follows on the heels of last year's Spanish language album *Mi Tierra* and represents Gloria's tribute to her favorite pop songs of the sixties and seventies—the songs that shaped her as an artist. The lead single from the LP, "Turn the Beat Around"—a cover of Vicki Sue Robinson's 1976 disco classic—is already making noise at pop radio and in the clubs. With "Everlasting Love" waiting in the wings, Gloria Estefan looks to be a fixture on the club charts well into the future. *DMA* talked with Gloria from Miami, where she was awaiting the release of her new album and the birth of her new baby.

Q: What made you decide to record an album of your favorite songs?

"A lot of things, really. In the back of our minds, all singers hope that someday we're in the position where we can do some of our favorite songs. It's kind of a tough position to get into because obviously the original music is what puts artists on the map and you have to maintain that. So, just the ability to be able to do this was a great thrill for me. We were going to do a studio album next after *Mi Tierra* and then do this afterwards. We had gotten the idea when we did a live concert for VH-1 called 'Center Stage.' They asked every artist to pick their favorite cover tune and do it, and we got such an incredible reaction from 'Hold Me, Thrill Me, Kiss Me.' My fans kept writing me—they wanted to buy this song. So, when I got pregnant, we really flip-flopped the album ideas. We thought this would be a great album to do while I'm pregnant because most of the pressure from an album is writing the material for me. Once that's done, it's okay. I wanted to be very stress free and to do something I really enjoyed that was fun and, at the same time, stay out there for my fans and give them something a bit different. *Mi Tierra* being one side of my roots and this being kind of like a soundtrack of my life in a way—songs from the pop charts through the years that influenced me in some way or that I really listened to."

Q: Tell us about the first single, "Turn the Beat Around."
"That was a real obvious choice for me because I think this was one of the first songs that really exploited the Latin percussion in disco. It was definitely a classic. It reminded me a bit of 'Conga' in the delivery of the words, and the horn section, of course, was very much like Miami Sound Machine. It was a record that we used to do a long time ago in the band and it was really a lot of fun to do. It was probably one of the first choices for the album."

Q: It's also on the soundtrack for The Specialist.
"Right. We were going to do this only for my album, but what happened was when we were mixing, Jerry Weintraub was in town with Sly, and Emilio told them that this song would be perfect for *The Specialist*. So, they came in and listened to it and they flipped—they loved it so much that they wanted it to be the first single. We did special mixes for the radio and for the clubs, and we did one with the movie in mind. It's not that we rerecorded anything, but we did a retro version and then a version that brought it a little more up to the nineties."

Q: That should help the record.
"Yeah. It's been doing great. Different stations play their favorite version. I've been hearing the retro version a lot. I think 'Everlasting Love' may be the second single. It's not etched in stone yet. They're fun songs to do. The mixers have a ball doing this stuff. We did it a little more energetic and also more into the nineties sound."

Q: Did disco music play a role in your development?
"Yes. You know, when disco started out, I was just starting in the band and we did a lot of these songs live. We were a gig band, so we did a lot of cover versions. It was something that

we did for fun. We never really intended for a career to happen. It happened very slowly. There were lots of songs we used to play—'Come To Me,' 'I Will Survive,' 'Turn the Beat Around.' It was the kind of thing that really fit the band well and it was a lot of fun to do. People used to love it. Then as we did more original material and less cover tunes, our songs became a mix of these influences. That music was great to dance to. People used to have a blast."

Q: Is it true that you recorded the album live in the studio?

"A lot of the songs were completely live. With 'Turn the Beat Around' and 'Everlasting Love,' we had different horn sections coming in at different times, but with a lot of the songs we wanted to capture the real intimacy of it—like the Neil Sedaka song 'Breaking Up Is Hard To Do.' We were all in there together because it was meant to have a very definite coffee house vibe, and the only way to get that really is to play it as if you were all playing it in one place. Many of the songs did end up being live, especially the songs of this era. They were all done live then. Technology wasn't at the point that it is now. They had a certain feeling that you can't recapture unless you do them in the same way."

Q: Did you choose all the songs yourself?

"Yes I did, but we were very democratic. The guys in the band gave me their ideas, but I wanted this to be something that was a choice of songs that really meant something to me because there were so many that are fantastic through the years that I would have wanted to do. But there had to be some criteria that tied them together because they were going to span different times. I wanted the one link to be that the songs were each in their own way very special to me. Some of the songs I used to play as a kid on my guitar for my friends like 'Don't Let the Sun

Catch You Crying' and 'Traces.' That's why we tried to capture that intimacy, too. Others were things that we did in the band like 'Breaking Up Is Hard To Do,' 'Turn the Beat Around.' Some have personal connections like 'Goodnight My Love.' Emilio and I were dating at that time, and there was a radio show that would close with this song every night and it just turned out that it was right before my curfew. So, he would end up bringing me home every night with this song playing. It really looks back to the beginning of our relationship."

Q: What's your personal favorite on the album?

"It's hard to pick a favorite. Probably in the running are 'It's Too Late' by Carole King and 'Don't Let the Sun Catch You Crying.' They express my personality a lot, what I love about music. 'Don't Let the Sun Catch You Crying' is very naked and organic and the instruments are very warm in a sparse arrangement. It's very special to me. I used to play that on the guitar and my friends and my family used to love it. It brings a lot of memories back."

Q: I could hear that one on the radio, too.

"It's going to be weird to see what happens because we'll have two singles, probably 'Turn the Beat Around' and 'Everlasting Love,' but after that I think most of the stations will just pick their favorite and play it. I really have no idea because we've never done anything like this before. It's kind of breaking new ground for us, and radio is at such a different point now. It's hard to predict, but I would love to hear that on the radio."

Q: Was Carole King a big influence on you?

"She was, and most especially the *Tapestry* album. I wore out two copies. As a writer and as a woman at that time, she sang timeless things and she wrote timeless things. Her music's still very relevant, and she has a very unique warmth and emotional character to her songs that I think, as a writer, really influenced me, too. She was very concise in her writing, and simplicity's one of my favorite things. She's definitely one of my big influences."

Q: So, when can we expect a new studio album?

"We were working on that before. I've written three songs and some of the guys in the band have several cuts. This album will probably be very early '96. We're planning also to tour sometime in the summer of '96. I really want to take some time off to have the baby and enjoy her. Really this next album will be crucial for us.

"It's been a long time since the last studio album. I really don't count *Mi Tierra* because that was a very special tribute. On the pop side, it's probably been since *Into the Light* back in 1991. It's an exciting prospect for us because we've really moved along so much in those five years personally and as musicians and writers. We're looking to take some of the things that we learned from *Mi Tierra* that we really loved and incorporate them into the new music. It's going to be very Afro-Cuban in its roots. It's definitely a step ahead and probably very different than any studio album we've done, but at the same time it's an evolution, hopefully, and a progression from all the things we've done through the years."

Q: You and Emilio had a great role in Jon Secada's success. Were you surprised at how successful he became?

"No, we weren't surprised because he really is a wonderful talent and even now he's just scratching the surface. He's the kind of talent that will be around for many years because he has so much to offer. Obviously, the beginning steps of any artist are rough because you have to establish a sound and a career. At this point, he's on his second album and he's doing very well.

He just started his tour. Emilio's in Mexico with him. He started last night—Latin America. But I knew that his voice and his writing—it's real—and I knew that the real things really come through. Through the years, he's going to surprise a lot of people. I think he'll stand the test of time."

Q: Are you working with any other new artists?

"Yes, actually Emilio is. I'm pretty much, at this point, taking a break. He's got a new label—Crescent Moon. He's signed six new artists, most of whom are on *The Specialist* soundtrack, and he's going to have some massive hits. He's really busy. He's a workaholic."

Q: What's it like to work with him?

"It's wonderful. People think we're together twenty-four hours a day, but it's really not the case. I go as little as possible to the office. They make me work when I go there! He's into a million things. We share everything. We talk about everything. I respect him a great deal. He's always the first one to hear my songs and I really respect his opinion. He's a great producer—wonderful to work with, really very open-minded, very democratic, the kind of man who motivates people. He's a real motivator."

Q: You've had great success on the dance charts. How important has the dance community been to your success?

"A very important role! In fact, my success in general came because of the dance market. Back in 1984, we did 'Dr. Beat,' which was on our seventh album for CBS International. This album was mostly in Spanish, but we had two cuts in English, and we really believed in this particular song, so we did the twenlve-inch ourselves. We went to Puerto Rico, which was the first time we worked with Pablo Flores, with whom we still work. He's a very talented guy. He had told us that he wanted to do this mix. We had heard him in a club in Puerto Rico do these incredible things with our songs in Spanish and we told him that if we ever did a twelve-inch we would like him to do it. He did a spectacular job. We threw that song on the B-side of our Spanish single and then we ourselves distributed it to all the clubs here in South Florida. Then somehow this record got exported to Europe and the next thing we knew it was number one in the dance clubs all over Europe. It actually went to Top-3 in pop all over Europe, and we were taken over there to do promotion and we did a follow-up English language album. And then Epic, in the States, thought we were a European band, so they tried to sign us and we told them we're signed to you already in your international division! When we were in Holland doing a promo for 'Dr. Beat,' we got the idea to write 'Conga' and actually wrote it on the way to London. So, the dance market has always been crucial for us. Then in the States, when 'Conga' came out—the clubs made 'Conga' before it ever got played on the radio because radio thought it was too risky. And because of the success of 'Conga' in the clubs, we were able to convince a lot of radio stations in the States to take a chance and play it once, and once it was played it would get an immediate reaction. All of this was pretty much due to the clubs both times on both continents."

Q: How do you feel about the current dance music scene?

"It's fantastic. I'm really not as into it as I was before, obviously, because of my lifestyle. We don't get to go clubbing much, but we're surrounded by the cream of the crop in these things—guys who do amazing mixes. Just the stuff that I've heard for 'Turn the Beat Around' is really eclectic and very different—each has its own style. It's exciting and more complex than it used to be before. We're talking about five different mixes each time— definitely a lot more work to be done. It's always exciting to do something on the edge because that's the first thing that people hear—the club records. They have a lot to do with what crosses to pop."

Q: Do you have anything special you'd like to say to your dance music fans?

"Well, I'd just like to say thank you for sticking with us through the years. I know we've been in and out. It's been ten years we're talking about almost, but when we've done the best on radio, clubs have led the way. Whenever we've had a success, our dance fans have had a lot to do with it and we really appreciate it."

Reprinted with permission from DMA *magazine, February 1995*

Artist Profile: Donna Summer

This interview focuses on the "First Lady of Dance Music"—Donna Summer. Donna's single, the Clivilles & Cole-produced "Melody of Love," has hit number one on the *Billboard* club chart, and Donna has been kept busy promoting her two new albums—her greatest hits collection, *Endless Summer*, and her holiday album, *Christmas Spirit*. Donna talks about her album of new material expected in the spring, her stature in the dance music community, her fans, her marriage, the rumors that she's "gone country," and much more.

Q: Who are you working with for your new album?

"I'm going to work with some of the people I've worked with in the past and then some new people. I'm holding songs from different artists. I don't know if she's available, but I'd like to write a song with Gloria Estefan, maybe with Amy Grant, and maybe Don Henley. I mean I don't know if these people are available. These won't necessarily be dance tunes, but they might be."

Q: Is the album going to be leaning dance?

"There'll be plenty of dance on there. I'm not thinking that the record's not going to be a dance album, but when you write so many songs, not everything can be 'bump 'n' grind.' At some point, even if it's a dance song, you want to start moving into some subject matter there. It gets boring after a while. So, hopefully writing with people who are coming from other places maybe you hit upon something really unique. That's what my hope is—not to not write dance music. By all means, it will be on the record for sure."

Q: What about these rumors that you've gone country?

"I went to Nashville because we write a lot of country songs that my husband and I don't sing. Actually, last year when I was touring around and doing some gigs, I sang a couple of those country songs on stage and some people were quite shocked. We write country songs, but we never get to perform or sing them. What we want to do is at least try to get other people to sing some of those songs we write because songs are like babies. It's sort of like you if you write a story. It means something to you and it will mean something to everyone if someone takes it and makes something out of it."

Q: Are you spending a lot of time in Nashville?

"Actually, in the last year and a half, I spent an exorbitant amount of time in Nashville. At one point, it was almost two weeks on and two weeks off. And then I started touring more and being busy with my record and that's sort of taken me out of every place. So, yes, I've spent a lot of time in Nashville."

Q: *Where do you live?*

"I live in Los Angeles. In Connecticut. I live in Newark, and I'll be living in Nashville. We want to get to get a house in Nashville that we like and then maybe we'll condense down to one house. You know, when you travel a lot and you see a lot all the time, you get tired of places. I'm not one of these kind of people who are very rooted in anything. I mean in terms of my living conditions, if I had my druthers, I'd live only in hotels and stay there until I got sick of it and move to the next hotel and I would never own a house. Then I'd always have room service and I'd always have someone cleaning up my room (laughs). I said to my husband that I'd like to see the whole world before I get too old to enjoy it. How can you do that? There's so much to see. That's the only way you could do it."

Q: *You and your husband have been together for quite a while. What's the secret of your success?*

"There's no secret. Struggling! Fighting! Yell it out! Scream it out! Get it out of your system. We're pretty volatile people. We allow each other the opportunity to not be perfect and yet we expect quality from each other at the same time. It's kind of an interesting relationship. We write together sometimes and we're together so much that we kind of can't stand each other. I don't mean that we hate each other, but you know how it is. I can't even explain it. I'm married. He's married. It's like 'For the rest of my life I'm stuck with you!' There's a sense of humor about it, but it's tough. It's not so much other people or getting involved with other people because that's really not the problem. It's negotiating your way with another person, incorporating their wants and their needs and your wants and your needs into your everyday life on a constant basis. It's really difficult. But, we're here. It's seventeen years later and we're happy."

Q: What about Stock/Aitken/Waterman?

"I was just with Pete Waterman and his new group of guys in London. They're writing a lot of stuff, so I went over there and wrote with them a little bit. I wrote one song that I really, really like a lot. It's really nice. I would like to write with Giorgio Moroder, too, but I don't want to write just another song with Giorgio. I would really like to wait until I'm in a position to do the whole album with Giorgio—to do a whole reunion album. I don't want to waste it on a one-off record, so maybe the next record after this would be good for Giorgio, or two records from now."

Q: Has the recent resurgence in seventies nostalgia been good for you?

"Really, I don't take too much advantage of that. I think it's good in terms of the fact that people are more aware of your music and of you. In that sense, I think it's good. But in terms of my person, I don't go and do nostalgia shows or anything. Though it's great when people are playing your songs and remembering you. What's not to like?"

Q: Do you like being referred to as the "Queen of Disco"?

"Oh, it's so nice being the queen! (laughs) The queen of anything! Yes, I love it! It doesn't bother me. It's kind of cute. My bodyguard for years refers to me as 'My Queen.' So, when other people hear him, he knows it's a joke, but people think that I want him to address me that way. It's not the case!"

Q: Are your most loyal fans are your dance music fans?

"I would think so. Definitely."

Q: You're almost worshipped at times within the club community.

"I don't want to be worshipped. I just want to be loved."

Q: Some of your fans can get pretty intense.

"Oh, yes, they can! I can attest to that! I've had some pretty intense fans."

Q: Do you feel a responsibility to continue putting out dance records because of your stature in the dance community?

"You know, it's not even a responsibility. It's a part of my history and heritage. I will probably always have dance songs on my records. It's my base. I don't think 'responsibility' is the right word. I think 'joy' would be a better word. I may not always be in the mood to make a dance song, but I am in no way rejecting that. There are times when I'm in a state of mind where I need to write a slow song. It's a fact. If I write a slow song, does that mean I'm not going to do a dance song again? I don't think so."

Q: What do you feel is your best album? Which one are you most proud of?

"I like the Christmas album. The *Bad Girls* album, I think, was a turning point for me. I think in terms of my own identity within the realm of my own career, that record was important to me. It may not be everybody else's favorite, but it had a lot of things for me that were little landmarks. In some ways, I'd have to say that album was it. There were other albums that weren't as successful. I love *Once Upon a Time*. It was just meant to be a little fairy tale album. I really wrote it for my daughter. Different records mean different things to different people."

Q: Will you be touring again?

"Well, I certainly hope so. I hope it'll be soon. I mean, I'm touring now, but in America, I probably will tour next year."

Q: It's been almost twenty years since 'Love To Love You Baby.' Did you ever dream that you'd be so successful for so long?

"No, I never dreamed I'd be this successful this long, but I always thought that I'd be in the business. I'd be getting my teeth replaced and I'd still be singing. I'll probably be like Lena Horne or somebody who's always there year after year. It'll be hard gettin' me out of here."

Reprinted with permission from DMA *magazine, January 1995*

Artist Profile: Ace of Base

One would be hard pressed to find a more impressive nineties pop music success story than that of Ace of Base. With their unique reggae-flavored dance pop sound, Ace of Base stormed the world, unleashing multiple hits over past three years in practically every country. The Swedish quartet's debut album, *The Sign*, has sold over eight million copies in the United States and an astounding twenty million worldwide. In fact, *The Sign* is the biggest-selling debut album ever according to the *Guinness Book of World Records*. The album generated four American Top-10 hits, including the title track, which *Billboard* ranks as the third biggest hit of all time. Grammy nominations, American Music Awards, *Billboard* awards, and countless gold and platinum records followed. Now Ace of Base returns with its second album, *The Bridge* (Arista), which finds Jonas "Joker" Berggren, his sisters Jenny and Linn, and their bandmate Ulf

"Buddha" Ekberg exploring new musical territory while retaining the hooks and harmonies that made the *The Sign* so irresistible. From the pulsating euro-influenced first single "Beautiful Life" to the Arabic-flavored "My Deja Vu" to the rich vocal arrangements of "Lucky Love," *The Bridge* proves that Ace of Base has only begun to reveal its creative potential. In the interview that follows, Ulf talks to *DMA* about the pressures of success, the band's club roots, the genesis of the Ace of Base sound, the annoying comparisons to ABBA, the new album, the old album, and more."

Q: *What have you been doing lately?*

"I was in South Africa and in London. I've been spinning around for about two months. I've been here since Saturday. I did an AIDS benefit Saturday and Sunday I did the VH-1 awards, and Monday and Tuesday we did a lot of promotion and Entertainment Tonight. Today it's a lot of press and promotion and tomorrow the same and then back to Europe for more promotion. We're going to record a new version of our 'Lucky Love' video—an American version. We're going to probably record that in Europe, but we haven't decided yet. 'Lucky Love' is the single out in Europe now, and 'Beautiful Life' was just released as the second single. 'Lucky Love' is being released here as the second single."

Q: *Why did you switch them for the United States?*

"Well, Americans always want to go their own way (laughs). No, actually they thought it was a better idea to shock the people with something, and I think it was a very good decision because it worked really well here. So, now 'Lucky Love' is a little bit more like old Ace of Base, so they're going to recognize us again. In Europe, they wanted to release 'Lucky Love' because they wanted them to know that this was Ace of Base.

It's another theory. It's very hard for me to say. I think they know what they're doing. Also, we have two different record companies. We have BMG/Arista here in America and we have Polygram/Metronome in Europe. They are two of the biggest competing companies in the world, so we have to work together."

Q: 'Beautiful Life' is more uptempo than usual for you—is it more dance?

"Well, actually that's really not true because when we started Ace of Base we were actually a house band. We played house music, so maybe 90 percent of our songs were uptempo—maybe 120 to 140 BPM. We just had two slow songs—'All That She Wants' (at that time it was called 'Mr. Ace') and 'Wheel of Fortune.' We had thirty house songs, but the record company preferred the slow songs, so we did more of these songs. On the first album, we have a few faster songs, too."

Q: The dance sound and the dance clubs played an important role early on?

"It did. In the start, it was the thing for us—to do dance music—not reggae music. All of us we love to go out and dance and party. The music's very important to us when we're going out and having fun and dancing. That's why it's very natural for us to do dance music."

Q: Do you think that the dance scene is as important as it was in the beginning for you?

"It's still very important, but before it was 100 percent. It can't be as important for us now. You always have to think about radio now. At that time, we tried to do music where the same version could work on the dance floor and on radio. Now we do radio versions and dance versions—totally different things—and also remixes. The dance scene is still very important to us. Junior Vasquez did a remix for us for 'Beautiful Life.' It was very important and very good. In Europe, we have a lot of really good remixers, too. Now we also have the opportunity to have really good people work with us and it's been nice."

Q: What inspired your reggae/techno sound—the 'All That She Wants' sound?

"I listened to Madness when I was young and much harder music like Skinny Puppy, Kraftwerk, Ministry, Front 242. I was at one of Front 242's first concerts in 1982. I was really with them in the start. I think there were a hundred people or something. I've seen Kraftwerk many times. I bought my first Kraftwerk record in 1979. So, that's a very big part of me. That's how I started to make music. My father bought me a computer in 1982—a Commodore 20—and I started to make music on it. When I bought the Commodore 64, I could use the MIDI system on it. It was a new era in 1984 and I started to do some—today you would call it techno—synth music with a danceable beat. That was a very natural way to work it out. We were ready to do this in Sweden. Back then when we did a lot of fast songs, but we wanted to do some slow songs. Jonas and I—at that time it was the end of the eighties—we liked the reggae sound, the beat, but not the production. We wanted to sound much clearer—a harder beat and a clearer sound, but still have the rhythm of reggae. So, we did something that we thought was good and that became what's now called the Ace of Base Sound, and 'All That She Wants' was the first song we did it on. It's African rhythms with a lot of synthesized sounds in combination with the reggae beat. That's how it came out.

"At that time, we didn't like the songs that were out. At the beginning of the eighties, we had all these disco/synth bands that pop radio were asking for—ABC, Depeche Mode, The

Cure—all that pop that came out there. We are from that era. At the end of the eighties, we thought 'Everybody lost it!' The only thing that was good was the dance music. Nobody could do better dance music than Snap, Blackbox, C+C Music Factory. These groups will be the best groups ever. Still, when I hear Snap, for example, I'm shaking. Nobody can beat this. Nobody. Something happened there. But on the lists, on the radio lists, something was missing. I thought, 'Where's the pop? Where's the melodies?' We had rock and roll, we had some kind of hip-hop with just rap—no melodies and these rock ballads, Bryan Adams. I thought, 'Where is the good pop eighties sound? It's nowhere!' So, we did the music we wanted to listen to ourselves."

Q: I think some people thought that that your sound wouldn't sell in the United States, but you proved them wrong.

"A lot of people thought that. A lot of record companies said that, too. Also, we had the opportunity to be with Arista—with Clive Davis. It's the best thing. He's the best guy in the world to do this. When he believes in something and he pushes buttons, it's happening. So, it was very good for us. Our first album sold actually twenty million copies worldwide! It's the biggest selling debut album ever. When I say the figures, it's like when I tell you my car is red, you know. I don't understand the figures, really. It's so big. It's like I'm inside a snowball rolling down a hill and the snowball's getting bigger and bigger and bigger, but I'm inside the snowball and I have to run the whole time or else I'll get killed. I'm running and running and running and I can't see how big the snow ball is because I'm inside it. When I reach the end and come out of the snowball, I can see how big it was. I'm now maybe starting to realize how big this is. The thing was for these three years, so much happened—all these number-one hits all over the world and all the huge sales, all the platinum records. After a while, you get filled up with all the information—you can't put anything more in-side. In the last year, when we started in the United States, we were filled with all this pressure. We were so confused. We were dizzy with all this success. We were just working and working and working. In 1993, I flew 179 times. I was more in the air than I was on the ground almost. It could be three countries in one day. In two days, we could play three different singles in different performances because we had four singles out at the same time in Europe. We released seven singles in Europe. When we went number one in the U.S., it should've been the greatest thing. We thought about how big it was for about five seconds, and then it disappeared. You couldn't imagine how big it was because you had too much going on. I'm really sorry for that because I really would like to have that feeling—'Wow. How is it to be number one in the U.S.?' We were in the middle of this dream—not nightmare—this dream—working, working, working, so we couldn't really appreciate it. It's very hard to ex-plain the feelings because the feelings were so confusing the whole time. Maybe if we're going to be number one again, I'll have a better explanation of how it feels. It's so flattering and so great."

Q: Did you feel a lot of pressure to top the first album?

"You know, the first album when we made it we had the suc-cess so fast, we had to finish the album very fast. We had all the songs—around forty songs. To put together an album in just a few weeks—it's a lot of pressure. We did one mix on each song and we couldn't even redo the mixes if we wanted to. We didn't have time to finish, so we had to put some of the demo versions we had recorded in our small demo studio on the album. We didn't have time to master the album—it was totally unmastered. With that knowledge, it's so good to have the time to think about the production and to really work and develop it. To have hit singles like 'The Sign,' it takes more than a very good song. You need a very good team around you. You need good timing and a lot of luck. This feeling of something new is gone now because we're not new anymore. So, we need something else. But all of us feel secure about the album because when you've done the best you could, you can't do better. The record company wanted us to work with a lot of producers and songwriters from all around the world, but we thought, it's too early to do that because we felt, 'We have to be secure. We have to feel comfortable when we write. It has to come from our heart and from our soul.' To make that happen we had to work with the same people we worked with on the last album. We had a lot of conversations with the record companies, you know—'You have to work with him and him and him and him.' The problem was everybody wanted to be involved because they wanted to tell people, 'Oh, I worked with Ace of Base. I made Ace of Base. I broke Ace of Base.' It seemed as if a thousand people made Ace of Base except for us. Too many people wanted to be involved. Too many chefs. In the end, they listened to us, so we did it our way. None of us feel pressure. We're more excited instead. It's like if you go out in a car race or a boat race or a tennis match. The adrenaline's pumping. You're going to do this. You're going to do the best now—100 percent."

Q: How has the sound changed since the first album?

"It's very natural to develop, and we had to develop since there are so many groups that copied our sound. I still think that none of them could succeed at copying us really because they're missing a few parts of it. Nobody did it really well, I think, but that's probably just my taste. It's natural to try and experiment with new things. The big difference is we used a lot of the acoustic instruments—guitars and also acoustic drums. I think we have a little bit more live feel to it. Also, another big difference is of course that the girls are writing now, too. So, we get another point of view—something that Jonas and I could never do.

Even if you write lyrics for the girls, you can never really have it from the girl's point of view. Girls think a little bit differently than boys—in different colors—another way of thinking of life. That's why I think it's really important to have the girl's point of view, and I've heard that from a lot of the girl fans we have out there. They may not be the hit singles on the album, but they're still very good album songs. It also shows that we are four songwriters in this group and that's unusual, I think."

Q: How do you feel about the frequent comparisons between Ace of Base and ABBA?

"I'm a little bit bothered by the question because we've had this question in almost every interview for three years (laughs). It's a very normal question, and I have the standard answer for that. Of course, it's very flattering to be compared to ABBA and I understand why—we are four people, we are from Sweden, we do pop music, two guys, two girls—one blond, one dark-haired. ABBA were pioneers. They did something very big and they were the first to do it. We're not pioneers. We may have done our own sound, but we're not pioneers. You know, Oasis is not the new Rolling Stones. Oasis is Oasis even though they're going to be compared with the Rolling Stones for probably five more years. We are Ace of Base—we are in the nineties. ABBA was in the seventies. It's a very big difference. The good thing was it opened up some doors. It made people listen to us. Also, in 1992, when we released the first album, it came at the same time that they released all these *ABBA Gold* collection albums. So, the ABBA thing had just come out. We came at the right time. I think it helped us a lot, but the question is starting to get a little boring. Because ABBA is so big in France and Australia, sometimes we've been on TV programs there where we're just talking for an hour about ABBA. It's like, 'Hello, ABBA doesn't exist anymore. Why are we talking about ABBA for an hour?'"

Q: How did you all get together?

"Jonas and I had known each other for a long time. We had the same music tastes. One of my bands shared a rehearsal studio with Jonas and his band and we started to work together in the studio and became really good friends. Then my band had a concert together with his band in 1990 in Gothenburg. We were playing outdoors and there were so many people. We performed first and one of the guys in Jonas' band jumped off— the keyboardist, so Jonas wanted me to join. I joined as a keyboardist in the concert that night and it was a big success. After that we started to write music together and we named the group Ace of Base."

Q: And the girls were there from the beginning?

"They were in the band with Jonas. That was the time when we started to work seriously on this. We felt, 'This is something. Let's go for this.' I rented my apartment and I lived in the studio for two and a half years. I was eating a pizza a week and hot bread and water. I put all my money, everything I had, each penny, into studio equipment and gave my time to be there working every day. I didn't even have a shower, so I had to walk twenty minutes every day to the Berggren family's house to take a shower. It was particularly hard in the winter when it was snowing and really cold. But it paid off."

Q: Are you happier now or were you happier then?

"I'm really happy now. Sometimes I think it would be fantastic to be a nobody—to do whatever you want and nobody cares. Like yesterday, two paparazzi were following me for one hour, running around and trying to make a scene with the camera in my face. My bodyguard put them away. It was a little bit annoying. I'm glad I didn't have a girlfriend with me because then it would be everywhere in the papers. It's annoying to have them looking into your life. You have to think, are they in the next window? Do they have microphones in my room? It's as if you have a big camera above your head the whole time and a microphone in your mouth. You have to think about what you're doing the whole time. But I love this life. Really I do. It's perfect for me. I love to travel around. I love to meet people, to do a lot of business. It's really fantastic. It's opened up so many doors. I've met so many people. I've met most of the people I really wanted to meet in my life. So, it really is a beautiful life. Hard, but beautiful."

Reprinted by permission of DMA *magazine, October 1995.*

CHAPTER THIRTEEN

Songwriter

B ecoming a successful songwriter requires not only talent, but plenty of hard work as well. Songwriting is the most creative of all the music business careers. The gratification that the success of one of your songs can bring to you can be unparalleled. One hit song can bring in royalties for years to come. So, in truth, one brilliant idea can set up a songwriter for life. Although this is rare, it happens. Witness songs like "Feelings," "Yesterday," "I Will Always Love You," "Cherish," and many more that become modern pop standards and that bring incredible income to the songwriters for a long time. Songwriters can earn income from the following sources:

- Mechanical Royalties (royalties directly from record sales)

- Performance Royalties (royalties from play on radio, TV, videos, movies, nightclubs, etc.)

- Sheet Music Sales

Many legal protections exist that make sure that the songwriter is paid for his or her ideas.

A songwriter combines music and lyrics into the magic of a song. The song forms the basis of the music business itself—the point where it all begins. Without the song, there is nothing for the artist to perform, no record to sell. Becoming a songwriter takes great patience, dedication, and hard work. One must be proficient enough at either piano or guitar to even begin, but, if you feel that you have the gift, then by all means pursue it. Whether you feel that you want to write music, lyrics, or both, songwriting can be a source of endless satisfaction, self-expression, and release, even if you never have one song published or recorded. Be sure that your motives are creative and not monetary, though. Great music is not born of greed, but of inspiration.

Giorgio Moroder, Songwriter

One of the great songwriting legends of our time, Giorgio Moroder, is responsible for such modern pop classics as "What A Feeling (Theme from *Flashdance*)," "Love To Love You Baby," "You Take My Breath Away," "I Feel Love," and many more. Because of his achievements as a record producer for Donna Summer and other dance artists in the seventies, Giorgio is widely considered "The Father of Disco." Giorgio won two Academy Awards for his work as a composer for the soundtracks to *Midnight Express* and *Top Gun*. Giorgio spoke from his Beverly Hills studio about the secrets of writing a hit song and his life as a composer.

Q: Could you tell us how you became a songwriter?

"I used to be musician and as a musician I basically worked in the evenings. So during the days I didn't have anything to do and eventually I bought a tape recorder and I started to compose for the piano. I played a little piano and guitar. Then I bought a second recorder a year or two later and I did some multitrack recording, like putting one track down and then copying it to the other machine, adding something new. I did that for about two to three years and then I tried to sell my material and basically I wasn't able to. Since I was traveling from city to city, I couldn't really sit down in a major city like maybe Paris or London and try to sell the material. So I decided to quit and with the money I had I was able to survive the first one to two years. So, by pure coincidence, I ended up in Berlin because I had an aunt there who helped me out. And I was quite lucky, one of the first songs I composed as an official composer, I was able to sell. Those three or four years really helped because I learned a little bit of technique—how to do better demos. Then I sold my first song. It was nice hit. We sold about one hundred thousand singles, which at that time was a lot. Then it took another three, four years to have some more hits. And then after about six, seven years I had my first major hit with Donna Summer."

Q: What's the secret to writing a great song?

"First I think the melody has to be a good melody—a melody that you can play easily on the piano and recognize as a melody. That's, in my opinion, a good melody. For example, if you take the songs of the Beatles, they all have great melodies. You play them and you know that song. If you take some of today's alternative rock songs, it's nearly impossible to play them because the song lives with the lyrics and the voice of the singer and it lives with that particular recording. If somebody else would try to record it, it would nearly be impossible. So I think the melody is the main ingredient."

Q: Can you learn how to become a songwriter?

"The better the education the more it helps. Sometimes the composer is too much into classical music or has learned too much. Sometimes it's a little bit of a drawback because then they are intimidated by doing things that are not within the classical parameters. Sometimes people who study fifteen years of music are a little shy, but otherwise the better you play an instrument the easier it is. But it really doesn't matter because

I started with guitar, then I played bass, then back to guitar, then gradually I started to play piano, but just enough so that I could compose. And it works out quite well."

Q: What do you like most about songwriting?

"First of all, I don't really enjoy it. It's always a painful thing because you have to sit down and have to come up with an idea. I enjoy the recording much, much more because then you know you hopefully have a good melody. The composing I never really enjoy. It's like the writer who has to come up with an idea. Once you have the idea, then it's okay. Sometimes it takes a whole day and nothing comes out, and sometimes it happens in a half an hour, an hour. But it's always kind of tricky."

Q: Are you writing all the time?

"No. Only if I have to. That's one of the things I learned, that it doesn't really work, at least for me, to sit down and just start to compose. I always want to know, have to know who it is, what kind of song it is, if it's a ballad or an up tempo, or otherwise it doesn't work. Most of the time when I just compose it's a waste of time."

Q: So your greatest challenge as a songwriter is coming up with the ideas?

"Yes, once you have a good melody then the rest, the arrangements, the recording are a lot of work, but it's easy because for the arrangements you use good musicians or come up with some good arrangement ideas. If you have great singers, of course, that helps. But the biggest obstacle is the composing. It's the most difficult thing to do."

Q: What advice would you give a young person who wants to become a songwriter?

"I must say it's getting a little more difficult than it used to be because now people in the industry—managers, producers, and A&R guys—they want to hear a good demo. Twenty years ago you could give them just a guitar and a voice, and maybe a piano, and they would recognize it and that's how everybody used to listen. Now they're all used to listening to nearly final recordings. So, for somebody to start, you need more money than we needed at that time. You need to have little bit of a set up where you can have programming software, at least a tape recorder, because in the industry, the people, they can't imagine like they used to how a song is going to be when it's done. So that's my first advice, to buy or rent or have a friend with a little studio and do good demos. And then the ways to go once you have a song are many. You can go to a publishing company, which is where I started, and give up some rights, make a deal for a period of time where they get all the songs and don't worry too much that you will only get your shares as a writer while the publisher gets all the shares of the publisher. If they do something for you, then they should make some money. Then, once you have a name, it's easier to get out of a deal, if it's not a good deal, or then, once the deal is over, to get a better deal."

CHAPTER FOURTEEN

Record Producer

G eorge Martin, Phil Spector, Giorgio Moroder, The Bee Gees, Phil Ramone, LA & Babyface, Jam & Lewis. These are a few of the legendary record producers whose names have become more well-known than many of the artists they produced. In the early sixties, when Phil Spector developed his patented "Wall of Sound," it signaled the beginning of an era of greater influence, fame, and success for the record producer. The majority of producers before Spector worked for record labels in a staff capacity and lacked the autonomy and creative freedom to develop in their own right. George Martin, the famed Beatles producer, worked on staff at Parlaphone/ EMI when he produced his first Beatles recording session. Martin went on to become one of the most innovative and influential producers of all time, overseeing several groundbreaking Beatles albums, including *Rubber Soul, Sgt. Pepper,* and *Abbey Road.* By the late sixties, producers were breaking away from the constraints of the record labels and working independently, forming their own production companies and paving the way for the future legends like Jam & Lewis, LA & Babyface, and Stock/Aitken/Waterman.

The record producer shapes the sound, feel, and direction of the record. He or she is responsible for capturing the "magic" that makes a hit. Often, the most successful producers (Jam & Lewis, LA & Babyface, The Bee Gees, Stock/Aitken/ Waterman) are prolific songwriters as well. In fact, in the case of the aforementioned, often the artists become interchangeable and sometimes forgettable due to the strongly identifiable songwriting/production style of these talented writer/producers. Stock/Aitken/Waterman were notorious for their need for control over their productions, and some artists actually complained about their lack of input on their own hit records. Nonetheless, Stock/Aitken/Waterman knew what worked and subsequently sent an unbelievable one hundred hits into U.K. Top-40 before they parted ways in the early nineties. Many times, successful producers get their start as artists. Jimmy Jam & Terry Lewis were members of the popular early eighties R&B outfit The Time, and LA & Babyface spent time in the mid-eighties as members of the group The Deele.

The songwriter/producer will usually start with a song of his or her own composed in the studio in demo form. The next step is to find a suitable singer/artist to record a final version of the song. It is the producer's responsibility to map out a vocal and instrumental arrangement, to hire musicians and background singers, keyboard and drum programmers, if necessary, and to book and guide the recording session so that the final product reflects the producer's particular vision for that record. Many producers are so self-contained that they play and program all of the instruments and even sing the background parts themselves. A prime example of this kind of producer is the multi-talented artist/producer Prince. Many artists like Prince and George Michael produce themselves. They are the rare talented few who do it all—write, sing, play, and produce—a far cry from the days of the staff producer!

Chris Cox, Record Producer

We interviewed up-and-coming producer Chris Cox of Interhit Records who, besides working as a co-producer with the legendary Giorgio Moroder, has had several hits of his own as a producer and is one of the new generation of producers who will be making hits into the next century.

Q: How did you break into the business?

"I started as a musician first. I've been playing instruments since I was about ten years old, starting in school bands and leading up to playing with bands in my hometown and doing local gigs and things like that. I've just been a complete fanatic about music ever since I can remember. I knew that was always what I wanted to do ever since I was young, so I basically worked all throughout high school and into college at trying to break into the music business. During high school, I became involved in any kind of musical activity I could, such as the school band, hanging out in the library and reading about music, record companies, and artists, and trying to absorb as much knowledge as I could about it, getting books in bookstores about how the industry works. I went to college on a music scholarship hoping to be a professional musician someday. I was working toward a performance degree as a jazz major at the University of Nevada, Las Vegas, and while there I was able to gain some experience in broadcasting. I started hanging around the campus radio station, KUNV. It had a jazz show on in the day time, and I was pretty proficient as far as my knowledge of jazz music and jazz players, so I did an air check and basically got a job working on the radio station. After a while I expanded my radio shift and started doing an alternative music show as well.

"Through working at KUNV, I started making a lot more contacts with different professionals in the industry, with promoters and different artists. What really got me into the aspect of producing was a class I took at UNLV in studio engineering. I knew that I wanted to work around music, and I knew that the studio was an integral part; therefore, I needed to learn more about it. So I took a studio engineering class and basically fell in love the whole aspect of the studio. As a live musician, there's that moment in time where you can create something beautiful. You can create something incredible, and unless it's recorded, it's gone forever and it will never be captured. What's fascinating about the studio is that you can not only capture a particular performance, but you can also create a performance that you hear in your head—something that would not be able to happen live. For instance, with a standard band, if you have four or five people who are playing, there are limitations to what you can accomplish. But when you get into the studio to start multi-tracking and overdubbing, you can create incredible soundscapes that you wouldn't be able to do live, and that was a turn-on for me. I like the experimentation of the studio and I like the studio atmosphere, the fact that it's a very controlled environment and you don't have to worry about dealing with patrons or dealing with weird smokey clubs and you can simply concentrate on the music itself in a very relaxed, very conducive environment for creativity.

"I made it my goal to work somewhere around the recording studio. As a musician I was okay, but I wasn't phenomenal. I knew I had a better talent at working with people rather than working with my own instrument. I felt comfortable enough as a musician, but what I really enjoyed about the studio was coming up with ideas and trying to help other musicians accomplish either what they wanted to do or what I could envision—in other words, using musicians as my instruments to create something entirely new.

"As far as particulars on how I got into the industry from there, I basically took a couple of classes and hung out with a few people in the studio who got to know me and liked the work I was doing experimenting with different musicians from that area. Meanwhile, the record company Hot Tracks had relocated to Las Vegas from the Bay Area and did not have a producer. They started inquiring around town about somebody who could take the place of their in-house producer, who had left. They were doing dance music and, at the same time I was working in the studio, I had also been a deejay and heavily into the nightclub scene. I had developed an interest in and a love for dance music. So when this company started asking around, my name came up several times as somebody to look into. Then I met with the owner of the label, played him tapes of things that I did, talked to him a bit, and got the job as the producer for this label. I didn't really feel that I knew everything that I should, but I knew enough to get going and, when it came time for the first couple of projects, it was like a crash course in finishing up what I needed to do to get to that stage.

"As far as the rest of it goes, it's been a steady climb. When I started working with the record company, I was fairly educated in the operations of the studio and had done enough projects to know what knobs and buttons did what, but I still needed a lot of fine tuning. That's something that I have found out since then—you never really finish honing your talents because, as you learn how to do something in the studio or as you learn how to develop a certain sound, there's always something else you end up learning along the way that opens another door for possibilities. After that experience as a producer, I started having a desire to find particular artists and do work with particular artists rather than simply doing projects that the record company gave me. I started developing tracks on my own, seeking out talent that could perform on these tracks and then shopping the tracks to different record labels as the producer. I can't say that I'm there yet as far as being where I want to be as a producer or where the possibilities lie, but at least I'm in a situation where I'm doing something that I completely love, which is producing, and I'm getting paid for it at the same time, which is quite remarkable."

Q: What skills and/or education does one need to become a producer?

"Well, as far as education, it's not like there is a "bachelor of producing" or anything like that. It's not necessarily an education that you need. There are certain courses that you can take. I myself took about three classes total in the art of studio recording, but a lot of that was more for engineering purposes.

It's good to learn what knobs and buttons do what because it's easier to communicate as a producer to the engineer or to other musicians through the terminologies commonly used in studios. So it's not necessary, but it is advised to at least take a course or find a way to be around a studio to learn the nuts and bolts of how the studio works.

"Education is obviously pretty important for just about anything in today's society. As far as a degree completion, it's not really any one degree that can help you as far as being a producer. A music degree can do one thing. A communications degree can do another. A management degree can even be a big help. I myself have two degrees in telecommunications and music, which well-prepared me for my work as a producer. The music degree obviously helped me to be able to communicate with musicians when working with them in the studio environment. The telecommunications degree helped me in the aspect of knowing, as a producer, what the possibilities are with the tracks I produce. In other words, the study of radio, the study of television, enabled me to know enough to be able to communicate intelligently with radio people, with TV people about the music I'm producing.

"As for the skills required for being a producer, communication would probably have to be number one. What you're doing as a producer is trying to take somebody else's raw idea and make it a finished product, or you're trying to convey your ideas of what you're trying to achieve with this track to other musicians or engineers or arrangers or songwriters. If you can't communicate those ideas, then you might as well do it yourself or forget about doing it. That's probably the most important aspect of working in the studio—being able to come up with an idea and relay it to other people so that collectively you can accomplish your goal for this particular project. You should have some skills for time management and organization. Organization plays a major part because, as a producer, it's your job to line up studios, musicians, engineers, singers, etc. It's a very important aspect because everyone needs to have the proper direction or the whole thing is going to fall apart. In the studio, it's advisable to have computer knowledge because almost all major recording studios nowadays are computer based, between sequencers, board automation, synthesizers, even studio management itself, with scheduling invoices, certain things like that. Just about everything is done on computer. There are some types of music—for instance, alternative rock or classical or jazz—that you're probably not going to be using computers as much. But for pop music and dance music, R&B and hip hop, you want to have some kind of computer skills because it's becoming a very vital part of the industry in those areas.

"In terms of other skills, you have to be very confident in yourself. You have to have some kind of assertiveness. A lot of being a producer is skill, but a lot of it is diplomacy. You have many instances where, if you're working with a band and the band is having problems within itself, the producer is the one who often has to be the mediator of these problems or sometimes even the babysitter. The producer has to keep control in the studio to accomplish a certain goal and should be very level-headed, but also somewhat assertive to gain that control. In the studio, the producer should command respect. It's not demanded or expected. Like the adage goes, you have to earn respect.

"Having the abilities, having the communication skills, and having the diplomatic capabilities of handling just about any situation are very crucial elements of being a producer. Without those, things could very well fall apart because people are relying on you, looking to you to lead the way, and expecting you to handle any circumstance. Almost all of the time, something will go wrong in the studio, and the producer is the one who has to gain control and to work out the problem. Other skills would be imagination and creativity because a lot of being a producer is trying to come up with new sounds, new ideas, new concepts, and exploring the different pathways that music can lead into."

Q: What exactly does a producer do?

"What a producer does is very much like what a director in a film does. A producer is the person who orchestrates the entire workings of the studio to accomplish one goal and that is to have a finished master recording. If you're using live instrumentation, the producer is often the one who will first find the song—either through a songwriter or often the producer will be the songwriter—and match it with a particular artist. Say, for instance, you have a female singer and you have a songwriter who comes to you with a song that may work very well with the singer. The producer is the one who has to determine if this combination will work before going into the studio and wasting a lot of time and money. A producer must have the vision of knowing what can work in the studio.

"The producer's responsibilities for completing a master recording vary depending on what type of project it is. If, for instance, it's a rock band, a lot of times the rock band will already have the song written, and the producer's first responsibility is to book an appropriate studio. If you know you're going to have huge guitar amplifiers, live drum sets, and multiple singers, then a producer will want to know the different studios in that area that would be appropriate for that band and also what kind of budget there is to work with to make sure that the band doesn't spend all of its money or all of the producer's money in the studio only doing part of the track without actually being able to finish everything. In a situation like that, with a live band, basically the producer is responsible for getting the absolute best possible performance out of that band, getting a comfortable environment for them. If the lighting is wrong or the temperature is wrong, a lot of times people have a hard time performing. The producer has to nurture the band members and take them by the hand and encourage them to give the best possible performance of that song. Then, at the point that you have that magical performance on tape, the producer is also responsible for determining, along with the band most of the time, if there are certain elements in that performance that need to be changed or added. In the end, the producer is trying to get the ultimate master recording of that performance."

Q: If it works that way for a rock band, what about for a pop artist?

"For pop music, the role of the producer has evolved and changed over the last fifteen years or so mostly due to computers. In the old days, producers would hire arrangers to write charts for live musicians, then hire the musicians to play the certain parts. In other words, if you were going to do a pop single, you knew you were going to need a bass player, a drummer, a keyboardist, a guitarist, and maybe a horn section. The producers had to know the best possible musicians in that area for that particular track. Nowadays, with the advent of computers, producers are usually working either with programmers or a good majority of the time doing a lot of the programming themselves. So they're not having to rely as much on arrangers and writing out music charts and often are not working with as many musicians. It really depends on the type of song."

Q: What do you like most about your job?

"The most amazing thing to me is the fact that I'm doing something that I completely love and I'm actually getting paid for it. Being a producer, working in a studio, working to create music is something that I'd be doing for free or even possibly paying somebody to let me do. The fact that you can make a living being happy or doing something that you love is very fulfilling. The other aspect of what's so amazing about being a producer is being able to create some great music, some music that you're very proud of. Like any art form, it's very gratifying when you start from nothing and, however long it takes, when you're done you have something that is immortalized. Even if it's a song that lasts three minutes, it's something that for that moment, for whoever's listening to it, it takes them somewhere else and you hope it can touch them. If you're trying to make some kind of statement or if you're trying to educate somebody or if you're just trying to entertain them for a brief few moments, it's very nice to be able to do that from scratch. It's like how a baker would make a cake out of ingredients that are insignificant when they're on their own, but collectively and using the right mixture of things and the right balance of things, the baker creates something wonderful. That's probably one of the most gratifying things of all."

Q: What's the most challenging aspect of the job?

"There are a few challenges. Probably the main challenge is dealing with the recording industry in general. It's very nice to be a producer—it's very nice to work on music and work with musicians, but the fact is, if you're not able to make a living at it, then you may not be a producer for long or you won't be a producer full-time because you'll have to have another job. Unless you have a hit and people are coming to you with every project in the world, there's a lot of work developing projects, trying to come up with sounds, trying to come up with the right artists and then once you have a package that you have finished in the studio, trying to get it to record labels so something can be released. That's the hardest part. At that point, it gets beyond just your talents in the studio and your talents as a musician or as a visionary. It becomes very political. It becomes very businesslike, and as a producer you have to wear many hats, in that respect, especially nowadays. A producer may be the one who not only discovers this wonderful talent, takes the artist in the studio, writes the song, records it, but then is also the one who has to be the salesperson to pitch it to a record label, so hopefully the project can get under a budget by the record company, get signed, and be able to do more recording.

"Staying fresh is another challenge. Very often, especially if you start getting really busy, you'll tend to do a lot of things the same way. Sometimes, as with any other job, you can actually get into a rut. You discover a formula to do a particular song and it seems to work, and then you get in a hurry and you end up doing it the same way every time. After awhile, it not only can be tedious, but it can also be very career threatening if people only expect that particular sound from you, from your recordings. It's a challenge to stay current with the music trends or to even be creating the new music trends and at the same time be a bit adventurous and a bit creative and still enjoy it. That's still a challenge because sometimes the other aspects of the industry can get you down and take you away from the bliss that you get from developing things in the studio. Sometimes it's a major challenge to stop worrying about that and to remember that you're doing it because you love music."

Q: What advice would you give someone who wants to produce records?

"The best thing to do is to set goals, but you don't want to set ridiculous goals at the beginning. There are many levels to the music industry and many levels to producing. A lot of people think, as I thought at one time, that you get a little bit of studio knowledge and you record a couple of tracks and then suddenly you're going to be a producer for life and make all the money and have all the gold records. That happens with some people, but for every one success there are probably at least a good thousand semi-successes or even failures. It's advisable to start at a lower level and really get your education in the studio, in music, in knowing how to how to finish a project before suddenly quitting your day job and becoming a record producer. There are a lot of aspects to producing—dealing with the people, dealing with the technologies, dealing with the politics. Until you have a minor grasp on a lot of that, you could end up putting yourself into some very uncomfortable situations, but also that's how you end up learning along the way. You need to have very thick skin. You will have recordings that people will hate. You will have rejections. Every major producer who's ever come along has had his or her share of rejections. Don't let it discourage you. If it's something that you truly love and something that you truly believe in, then you'll be able to do it.

"There are so many different types of music. There are so many different avenues to go down as a producer. If you find that one isn't successful, don't let it discourage you. That's probably the main thing. Most of being a producer is having the confidence, not only in the people around you, but in your own abilities because people will see right through it if you're not confident. Therefore, if you do get discouraged and do get distracted from the goal, it may not work out for you.

"Always pay attention when you're in the studio to the other people around you because, even if you are the producer in that session, there's always something you can learn from the other musicians, from the engineers. Every time you work in a session, imagine that you're going to school again because every session you do can be another lesson. You need to absorb everything you can because something that you learn in that session most likely you'll need to call upon later at another session. So, be ready for criticism, but don't be discouraged by it. Pay attention, and try to soak up all the information you can about the workings of a studio and it can be a very enjoyable career."

CHAPTER FIFTEEN

Recording Engineer

*I*f you enjoy the technical side of the recording process, if you like working with computers, if you are fascinated by electronics, if you love the mechanics of sound, a career as a studio engineer may be your ticket to success. Not everyone who has an interest in music and the music business wants to be in the spotlight. Many behind-the-scenes players make a significant contribution to the success of a record, though the general public many be completely unaware of who they are or what they do. The studio engineer falls into this category.

Today's recording studios are complicated and technically challenging environments compared to the simplicity of the early days of studio recording. Increasing reliance on computer programming, computerized mixing consoles, and the MIDI system make the studio engineer more important than ever. Often a producer will depend heavily on the talents of the engineer to achieve that perfect sound the producer is seeking. The engineer possesses the experience with the mixing console and outboard equipment, such as digital delays, reverb units, compressors, limiters, and much more to help create a great-sounding record. The studio engineer's familiarity with the technical aspects of the recording studio make the individual an extremely valuable asset to a project. The record producer needs to focus on supervising the session and getting the best performances out of the musicians and singers. The producer does not want to have to worry about what wire is plugged in where and what knob is turned which way. This is the engineer's job. The engineer keeps the session running smoothly and, in case of technical difficulty, is able to handle a variety of problems quickly and efficiently.

Often an engineer starts at the bottom in the studio, possibly answering phones, cataloging tapes, and running errands. Next may come a second engineering position and then, after gaining enough experience and knowledge, the coveted position of first engineer. After success working for a studio as a first engineer, often free-lancing is next, with the flexibility of making your own schedule, your own hours, and being your own boss. To get to that point takes a lot of hard work, long hours, and being at the right place at the right time.

Brian Reeves, Studio Engineer

One engineer who has reached that point is studio veteran Brian Reeves, whose credits include engineering on records for artists such as Donna Summer, The Pet Shop Boys, and Billy Idol.

Q: How did you break into recording engineering?

"In 1977, I moved to Los Angeles from Sacramento and I was pretty determined that that's what I wanted to do. It definitely wouldn't have happened if I didn't really want it. I started by going around from studio to studio and filling out applications, and it was pretty frustrating. I didn't really get anywhere with that. At that time, in '77, there were no schools, nothing accredited as there is now. I had a friend who was an engineer, Baker Bigsby. He does a lot of jazz albums. He was working at Fantasy Studios a lot of the time and I hung out at sessions with him. Basically, his advice was to work at a studio where the clientele is top notch so that you wind up ultimately working with great clients. If you work at a lesser-known studio, you might be a first engineer sooner and you might be running the sessions sooner, but what sessions will you be running? You might not be engineering the most happening sessions in the world—maybe more demos and things like that. So, I started to focus on the major studios and I really hammered at Westlake Audio and finally got a job there. They were building a couple of new studios, and I got a job as a laborer doing construction. I learned a bit about how studios are built, how sound-proofing is done, and how preparation for wire runs, like troughs in the floor, is thought through.

"Then when the studio was all finished, I got laid off and had to get another job. About half a year later, through more constant persistence—calling them up and going over there—I got hired again. Westlake Audio not only was a studio, a functioning recording studio, but it was also a retailer and sold professional audio equipment and contracted to build studios. So, I was doing a lot of the retail delivery and service pick-ups and things like that—driving a van around town in Southern California and picking up gear and delivering gear. I got to meet a lot of other studio owners, and that's why I started to question whether or not I should really stick with Westlake.

"I had a couple of offers to come and start doing assistant engineering at lesser-known studios, but I remembered what Baker said and I stuck with Westlake. I had an opportunity at that time—while I was driving this truck around—I had permission from the management to use the studio when no one else was using it, when the board wasn't set up and the studio wasn't locked out. I could go in there and do whatever I wanted. Generally the hours that the studio was available were usually sometime around two or three in the morning till eight. So, I used to go home and go to bed and then get up really early, like at four o'clock, and go to the studio for a few hours every morning before I went to work driving the truck. And I basically got an education. I went in there and got stumped with certain things and got manuals and read them and then asked questions of the technical staff.

"By the time an opportunity came along to be an assistant engineer, they were basically vacillating between either having an experienced second engineer come in, who might need some time to learn the rooms and find out where all the gear is and how everything's hooked up and patched in and how the board works, or me. These days everywhere you go it seems as if there's an SSL or a Neve. The studios are pretty generic compared to then. Then there was a wider array of equipment. Now you actually have independent second engineers who go from studio to studio, and because the studios are so similar and the patch bays and the equipment are all so similar, they're able to adapt pretty well. Back then, though, the studios were more of a collage of different odds and ends, and to get an outside engineer, even though he or she may have been experienced, to become familiar with those particular rooms would've taken some time. So, instead they chose me. I didn't have any experience, but I was really familiar with the rooms because I'd been spending all those early mornings in there for the last year.

"I got stuck working with Giorgio Moroder because nobody else wanted to (laughs), and it didn't take long for me to move up. The guy who was engineering for him then was also arranging for him—that was Harold Faltermeyer and Harold needed a lot of help on the engineering end. So, in my first second engineering job I was already doing a lot of first engineering tasks—a lot of the stuff that the engineer would normally handle. I stayed on staff at Westlake as a second engineer for maybe a year or so and then I went independent. With Giorgio and other clients, I had enough of a client base that I didn't have time to do any more second engineering.

"These days it's quite a bit different getting started. I think most assistants I've worked with in the last five years are college graduates and have degrees from accredited colleges in audio engineering. That didn't exist when I started, but even though they have that education, they basically have to start out doing similar things to what I did—maybe not delivering equipment from studio to studio, but Record Plant, for example, needs people to park the cars and run for meals and answer the phones. Even the guys who are graduates of Full Sail Recording in Florida or some of these other accredited courses start out parking cars and running for meals for a year or two. Then, depending on their personalities and the opportunities that they may or may not walk into, they move into second engineering and it's pretty easy to get a client base. If you're working in a place like the Record Plant, you're going to be working with great people."

Q: What skills and/or education does one need to make it as a recording engineer?

"I think the education that you get at one of the accredited places that I'm talking about is a good basic education, but I think that the skills you need are quite often people skills because you're not dealing with bankers and lawyers and government workers. You're dealing with artists and producers who tend to be very passionate about what they're doing. The hours get ridiculous and sometimes the attitudes get pretty insane based on the passion that they have for what they're doing. They're unusual people. So, I think that being able to cope with that or being excited about that or having fun with that is part of what you've got to have.

"I think you have to be motivated. I think you really have to love music and I think you really have to enjoy the technical aspect of it. It has to be fun for you and you have to want it because, even with the education, you're going to wind up going through a lot to get into the recording studio and then, once you're in the recording studio, it's going to take a lot of hard work to advance.

"Once you start working in the studio, you begin to learn from experience. I think there are a lot of creative people out there who present you with a lot of interesting new angles on tasks at hand. I don't know what kind of curriculum these colleges have, but often there are things you can't learn in school.

"I watched a guy editing in Munich—this old German guy—and he edited the tape with a pair of scissors while it was moving at fifteen inches per second on a tape machine. He'd be tapping his foot along and you know he had his point in the tape path where he would reach in and just go "snip" on the beat and he'd let the tape roll down and he's snip it again and then he'd just pick it up and wrap it around and continue to play or maybe fast forward and then play and edit. Then, while he rewound the tape, he'd stop and tape all the splices together and then before he did anything else he'd run a copy! I mean without even listening to a single edit, and it was just perfect. You know I thought that was pretty radical, drastic, fast editing. I've seen people really triple and quadruple check themselves before they even mark the tape to cut it and this guy didn't even bother to mark it and it gave me a different viewpoint about editing than most engineers have. Most engineers don't really see it that way. They see it as being something that you have to be a little more cautious and meticulous about and maybe that's good, but on the other hand, maybe it's not always necessary. There's different criteria for what speed you're going to work at and what the purpose of the product is and what the budget is and what the deadline is. These are things that you find out about in the real world that may be quite a bit different than what they teach in school."

Q: What does a recording engineer do?

"You set up microphones, you plug in instruments, you note the signal flow on the desk, you route things to tape, and you assure that the quality of what comes from the microphone is good. You assure the quality of everything that gets recorded to tape. You assure the quality of what gets routed through the board and played back and then ultimately mixed down to another two-track medium, or whatever medium. If it's movies it might be six or eight or twelve tracks or whatever you're mixing to. So it's quality assurance and it's also trying to help creative entities like producers and artists realize their sonic vision. So, you may have to translate certain terminology or phraseology from creative people into some sort of piece of gear that's going to make that happen. I had Donna Summer always asking for more sustain on her voice. Well, what does that mean? What it turned out to mean was reverb. She wanted to hear her voice ring out in a reverb. Sometimes people have trouble because they're very dynamic singers and, if they sing in the low part of their range in the verse and then have a more powerful section in the chorus, they have trouble hearing themselves in the verse. You can remedy this by compressing the vocal and/or riding the playback level or the record level for them while they're doing it and just kind of helping things along—trying to make the technical aspect of making a record as transparent as possible for the creative person and assuring the quality along the way. I think the better engineers, the more musical engineers, the real "big ears," eventually do develop great judgment in mixing and in production and become "one" with the technical and the creative side at the same time."

Q: Is it common for engineers to become producers?

"It's not uncommon, let's put it that way. There are a lot of career engineers who will never be producers, but I think that for many, many engineers it's a logical step. For some, it's not really. They're more in touch with the technical aspects of things than they are with the musical, although they may grasp all of the musical and creative things that are thrown at them and do well in translating that into whatever technical task is required to make it happen creatively, but that doesn't necessarily mean that they come up with the production ideas. Still, a lot of people who get into the business of engineering get into it because they love music and they have a tendency to be creative and have creative ideas and to be musical anyway. So it's a pretty natural extension of engineering to get into producing."

Q: *What do you like most about your job?*

"The music. I love the music. I appreciate all kinds of music. I like the "ear candy" aspect of records. I like when it sounds really good."

Q: *What is the most challenging aspect of your job?*

"I would say that sometimes the hours are pretty challenging. Sometimes because of deadlines it gets pretty ridiculous. For the most part I get along great with the people I work with, but every once in a while I'll get into a session where there's obviously incompatible personalities. Although that's only happened a handful of times in my career, it seems like an impasse when it happens. When it has happened it's been impossible to get around. But definitely the technical stuff is no longer a challenge. The typical sessions are really easy and even the complicated sessions—it's not overwhelming anymore, and that was a nice threshold to cross when I did."

Q: *What advice would you give someone who wants to break into recording engineering?*

"Be prepared for some dues-paying, and be prepared to learn a lot from professionals who have been doing it for years. There are a lot of different ways to skin a cat, so to speak. Ultimately everybody's trying to make a record or do something sonically creative or musically creative, but there are so many different ways to look at things and it's so subjective. It's good to keep a very open mind. For me, even after doing this for almost twenty years, I'm constantly reminded of how many different ways there are to do it. It's interesting still and I am still learning.

Having a degree doesn't necessarily mean that you've really begun to learn about the creative process. You may have a good handle on the technical aspects of it, but you've got to integrate that into the personalities and the hours and the deadlines and the pressures and the creative aspect of it, too. If you're working with an artist whose every vocal line is precious and the producer and other people in the control room make you acutely aware of that, it's a lot of stress getting ready to punch in. Then other producers and artists are so loose that you don't feel that kind of pressure. It varies from session to session."

CHAPTER SIXTEEN

Remixer

A relatively new field of opportunity on the creative side of the music business is that of remixing. In recent years, dance remixes of pop and alternative records have played a big role in the success of those records. In the past ten years, the industry has recognized the importance of the dance community in the development of a hit record and consequently those with the talent to remix records for the dance floor have taken on a whole new level of importance themselves. Dance remixes help to expose pop records to the club community with the end result being more records sold. Often club play sells records and, if you hear a great record while you're at the disco, you may just run out to the record store the next day and buy it. In other words, the dance remix helps the record reach an audience that it would not normally reach. Remixes are often done of several different styles of dance music in order to appeal to all the different types of clubs and clubgoers out there. One may find on the new Madonna single a "house" mix, a "techno" mix, an "underground" mix, a "trance" mix, and the list goes on and on. Sometimes there are so many mixes done that they don't all fit on one record! Hence, the recent popularity of "double packs," where you get two twelve-inch records instead of one.

It's often a matter of course that the major stars like Madonna, Mariah Carey, Whitney Houston, and George Michael commission dance remixes when they release a new single. These stars are able to pay the high prices to get the hottest remixers to remix their record. The highest-paid and highest-profile remixers these days include Junior Vasquez, David Morales, Frankie Knuckles, Armand Van Helden, Richard "Humpty" Vission, Eric Kupper, and others. Many of the in-demand remixers command up to $15,000 per remix—work that usually takes a couple of days to complete. Getting to that level is not easy. It takes years of hard work, dedication, talent, and an affinity for dance music. Many remixers start out as club deejays. Some begin as musicians, others as recording engineers. Remixing today entails a good knowledge of computers and the patience and willingness to work with the programs with which digital remixes are created. More and more remixing is becoming a computer exercise rather than a studio exercise. A remixer can take a vocal track, load it onto a hard drive, and create an entirely new record without ever leaving the computer!

Chris Cox, Remixer

One of the bright rising stars in the field of remixing is Chris Cox. Chris served as producer of Hot Tracks—one of the leading remix services in the United States—for over five years before striking out on his own as a remixer and producer. Chris's remixes of Donna Summer, Paula Abdul, 2 Unlimited, Outta Control, and many more have ignited dance floors across the country for the past several years. In the interview that follows, Chris talks about the world of remixing from the inside out.

Q: How did you get into the world of remixing?

"While I was going to college and deejaying on radio stations, I started working as a mobile deejay, playing music for weddings, parties, dances, and proms. That was in the early to mid-eighties, and beat mixing had started coming into play where a lot of the deejays would overlap one record with another and match the beat to keep a continuous flow of music, so the people would never want to leave the floor. I started doing mobile gigs and I did those for a couple years. While I was doing that, I basically taught myself how to mix records. I also got into the structure of dance music and the dance music sound and the dance music scene. I was good enough that between the radio station I was working at, which was the college station KUNV, and doing my mobile music, I was overheard by a few people and got an opportunity to deejay at a nightclub. That is where I really got into the whole scene of dance music and actually learned what remixing was. Then I started becoming a higher-profile deejay in the market. I was working about six or seven nights a week, about eight or nine hours a night, and completely living dance music. At the same time, I was studying as a musician at the university and not necessarily enjoying the type of music that I was studying there. I was enjoying more what I was doing at the nightclubs.

"So, I learned early on from reading and from listening to records that remixing could be the one thing that could mesh what I knew about music and what I knew about nightclubs and dance music. It seemed like a logical step for me because I had a love of music, I had a love of the recording studio, but I also had a love of the night life—of nightclubbing and dance music in general. I hooked up with a deejay remix service called Hot Tracks, which had been around since about 1981. They take songs or dance tracks or even regular pop tracks that aren't really made for the dance clubs or the dance deejays and alter them either by editing or remixing them, so deejays can mix the records more easily. I became Hot Tracks' producer and did that for over five years.

"I began by editing tracks—taking a track that was a three-minute track and editing it into a six-minute extended remix where you add the breaks and the structure that the deejays need to be able to beat-mix the records. After a while, my work began to gain notice and I started getting some higher-profile offers as an editor. I continued to learn more about the studio workings and eventually got more into remixing. By the nineties, I was remixing the tracks for labels all over the world and having my records heard in many, many nightclubs."

Q: What skills does a remixer need?

"The main skill that a remixer needs is a knowledge of what the club deejay is looking for. It's not enough just to have the technique of how to operate the equipment that you use to do the remixes. You have to know what your end result is going to be, which is a record that any club deejay can use. It's got to be properly structured for them, so they can work it into their sets, and it's got to have the right sounds that fit into whatever genre that you're remixing for. Therefore, the skills would have to be a knowledge of the dance music industry, hopefully a little bit of history on dance music and, especially nowadays, the skills in the recording studio and with computers. Probably about 95 percent of all remixing nowadays is done on computers. So, having a knowledge of the main programs for sequencing, for sampling, for digital recording, and for editing all comes heavily into play in the remix world. It also helps to have skills as a deejay as well so you know who you're creating your product for. It's nice to be able to know how to mix the records and how to use all the deejay equipment because that is your end market."

Q: What exactly does a remixer do?

"What a remixer does is take a track and make it fit the sound and the style of the dance music scene. The theoretical aspect of what remixers do is that they're taking a song, say a regular pop song or a rock song that wouldn't necessarily be played in a dance club because it doesn't sound like a dance record, and making it into a dance record by altering the music, adding new music, taking certain tracks out, doing whatever it takes to make the song accessible for the dance music deejays. In the dance music community, styles vary from city to city and, especially in the United States, from region to region. New York is going to play different dance music than L.A. or Miami as opposed to somewhere in Nebraska. So what a remix can do a lot of times is make a record more marketable by making it more accessible in a particular geographic area.

"There are so many different types of dance clubs and different types of deejays. A remixer can take one record that works for one set of deejays and modify it to fit another style and another sound. In the old days, in the disco days, what a remixer would do is take the original tracks of a dance record and simply mix them down again, run the multiple tracks through a console, alter the balance of things, and actually do another mix-down of the record. That's where the term 'remixer' came from. They would remix the record differently from how the original master recording was mixed. Then it evolved to where the remixer would edit in longer breaks to create the deejay structure and extend the versions.

"Nowadays, the term remixer has taken on a totally different aspect. What a remixer does most of the time is to reproduce the track or even sometimes rewrite the track to where they take an existing track, use only some of the elements from the master tapes, and then also *add* other tracks. Say you have a rock track and guitars weren't really acceptable in the types of clubs where you want this record to be played. The remixer would then take the lead vocals, take maybe a keyboard line or two, take out the guitars, take out the bass, take out some of the drums and then add in new tracks to alter and modify the song so it would work in a dance environment. A lot of remixers nowadays will just take the acapella of the track and basically rewrite the entire new track around it and rearrange or reproduce the track to make it an entirely new product."

Q: What do you like most about remixing?

"Remixing is really fun because it's a great creative medium, it's a great creative canvas. One of the hardest things about songwriting and producing is coming up with that original idea. What's fun about remixing is taking the original idea and seeing what kind of variation you can make of it and sometimes testing to see how far you can go before it becomes kind of ridiculous. Being a remixer is fun because you're able to create a piece of product—especially if you're a deejay who's gone into remixing—to create product that you can play or you would play if you were deejaying. It's a very gratifying kind of work to create product that you would enjoy yourself.

"Much like other aspects of the recording industry, it is a creative medium and it's a very enjoyable way to hopefully make a living and do work that you're proud and at the same time. Since dancing seems to be one of the most exciting means of self-expression and of entertainment, it's gratifying also to see the entire dance floor of people go completely crazy over something you did. It's fun to see people who already know an existing song in its original form hear the modifications that you made, hear an entirely new version that you've created, and enjoy it. Sometimes there are people who don't like a song in its original form for one reason or another and after you're finished with it then suddenly it's a song that they really enjoy. That's very gratifying."

Q: What's the most challenging aspect of remixing?

"The most challenging aspect of remixing nowadays is just getting into it and being able to make any kind of money. Since the late eighties and nineties, remixing has become very popular. Almost every deejay is trying to get into the world of remixing, so it's become a very competitive market. Dance music in general is often looked down upon in the music industry, and sometimes it's difficult to get the proper budget and support from the record labels that a remixer needs. Since there are so many people trying to get into remixing and since it's done often on shoestring budgets, there are many people who do it for free or for close to nothing, and the record labels often utilize those people first. People who are trying to do remixing for a living sometimes aren't able to get as many paid jobs as they would like.

"Another problem with remixing is that dance music comes in a series of trends and a series of waves of styles. Therefore, if you're a remixer who specializes in a particular style of dance music, after that trend is over in a year, year and a half, then suddenly you are not able to find work or you have to alter your style to fit the newer sounds. Dance music is probably one of the most rapidly changing styles of music in the industry, and it's something that takes a lot of work to keep up with."

Q: What advice would you give someone who wanted to break into remixing?

"Like other aspects of the industry, the main thing is not to get your hopes too high. Don't expect to make a lot of money at first because the remixing field is seldom a very high-paying field. Normally there will be a few people in the industry who command very high salaries because they're sitting on top of all of the hit records. With the hundreds of other remixers breaking into the field, it's often very hard to get paid by record labels. Therefore, going into the industry be prepared for the worst because then you won't be disappointed if something goes wrong. Make sure you have some kind of steady source of income. If you are still deejaying, it's a good idea to keep deejaying because you stay fresh on the sounds, plus it also gives you a good place to try out the recordings and the remixes that you are doing or that you have done. It's a good idea to stay there for a little while until your name becomes big enough or until you become stable enough as a remixer to rely solely on that.

Pay a lot of attention to the other records in the market or in the style that you prefer. Sounds change quickly in the dance music world and it's advisable to stay on top of that, otherwise you can sound dated in a matter of months.

"Other advice is to have a good knowledge of recording studio operations and especially the tools that are used by the remixer, which are primarily computers, samplers, drum machines, synthesizers, multitrack tape units, other things like that. Have a knowledge of those because too often, especially under a deadline, you'll have to know how to get a particular sound or you'll have to be able to work under a time constraint and, without that knowledge and that background, it's very likely that you'll end up missing a deadline or not putting out a piece of product that is as exceptional as the record labels would like it to be and therefore you will not get called for the next job.

"It's also advisable to be very visible. Learn how to promote yourself as a remixer. Learn how to keep in contact with record label people, with artists, with managers—anyone you deal with in the industry. Keep in contact with them, follow-up with them. While you're getting started at least, constantly circulate tapes of your work to different people. It's a good thing if you've done a few records to keep in touch with deejays in your market and let them know what you're doing. Take them copies of the records so that they can play them in their clubs. The more your name is spread around, the better chance you'll have of getting called for the next job. Keep your music fresh. Keep it exciting without getting into a rut. Try not to do the same thing over and over again on many records. It's kind of a catch twenty-two. You want to have a distinctive sound so that record companies know they have to call you in order to get that sound, yet you don't want to constantly have everything sound exactly like your last record. So, you want to evolve, you want to be creative, but at the same time you don't want to be redundant, which is often the case in the dance music industry."

CHAPTER SEVENTEEN

Artist Management

I f you have a strong interest in the business of music, but don't necessarily want to be the star yourself, artist management may be for you. Entry-level jobs in artist management range from receptionist at one of the high-powered, high-profile management companies such as Gold Mountain, DeMann Entertainment, or Gallin/Morey to being your own boss and managing a band at your school or college. Of course, being a manager of a struggling young band or artist may be a struggle in itself (and you most likely will have to work a second job to pay the rent), but the rewards and personal satisfaction of seeing your band or artist succeed can certainly outweigh the hard times. A safer route, of course, is to seek employment at an established management company and work your way up the ladder. This way you get to work with and learn from those with a wide range of experience in artist management, plus you get to meet the stars! Either way, be prepared for a lot of work, travel, and excitement. After all, this is where the stars are made *and* maintained!

The artist manager is the most important person to an artist. Artists depend on their managers to guide their careers, to protect them from bad deals and unscrupulous people, and to help them to fulfill their dreams. Artist managers often help with major career decisions, such as which record company to sign with, what publisher to go with, how to invest money, and when to go on tour. They also assist in the creative process by helping to select producers, choose songs, or hire musicians. Managers can be a great source of contacts as well. They can introduce artists to lawyers, business managers, road managers, agents, publicists, promoters, and others who can best further an artist's career. A good artist manager will work closely with the record company to coordinate advertising, publicity, and marketing campaigns for the artist's records, and a good manager will make sure that the record company does its job properly. All in all, the artist manager serves as a buffer between the artist and the outside world and for all of these efforts usually earns between 15 percent and 20 percent of the artist's income.

Kenny Laguna, Artist Manager

An expert in this field with a world of experience is Jett Lag Management's Kenny Laguna, manager of the well-known rock artist Joan Jett. In the interview that follows, Kenny gives us great insight into the field of artist management and realistic, practical advice for those contemplating artist management as a career.

Q: How did you break into artist management?

"Originally, I was a keyboardist and vocalist for a lot of 'bubble gum' bands that had hits in the late sixties—Tommy James and the Shondells, 1910 Fruitgum Company, Ohio Express, and others. Then I gradually came to be involved with Bill Medley from the Righteous Brothers. I made a few records with him and Darlene Love and expanded my horizons a little bit. Then bubble gum died in about a week, and the way our business works there was nothing available for me. Guys who I'd made millions of dollars for wouldn't even let me work in the mailroom. So that was a bit sobering.

"What happened then was I got a shot from a guy who was the original manager and producer for The Who, when they were called The High Numbers. His name was Peter Meade. He brought me over to England. I'd always been producing records even when I was doing bubble gum, but in England I became a producer who would actually join the band. This was right when punk music was happening there and I was having a lot of hit records in England. I would become a member of the band, the extra member of the band. Most of these bands didn't even have a keyboardist, so, because that was my specialty, I was able to affect their music, the arrangements, and then do the necessary keyboard parts and vocals. That ilk of band didn't really do background parts the way they did them in New York. I grew up with a lot of the do-wop bands, with Dion and the Belmonts and Elvis, who had great backgrounds.

"So that became a career. I became a record producer, and I was doing well at it, in my own little niche. I did a lot of the Bezerkley records. I was working for Leiber and Krebs, helping them pick the singles for their heavy metal bands. Then in the late seventies, when punk music was at its peak, I was approached by the management for The Runaways to do a record. I ended up doing Greg Kihn instead.

"Maybe a year later I heard from the Runaways' manager that Joan Jett needed help on a project. I was introduced to Joan, and we had to write ten songs in a weekend. We did that and I became really impressed with her. I said, 'This girl could have hits. We can do a whole thing with her.' I really saw what could be. Sometimes you see what could be and you're wrong. She came to me with 'I Love Rock N Roll,' but nobody really saw the wisdom of it. She had a version that she had done with the Sex Pistols, and we had that as a demo. Then she had a falling out with her manager, and I connected her with Leiber and Krebs, who, at the time, were the biggest managers in the world. They had Aerosmith, Ted Nugent, AC/DC, Motley Crue—they had everything. Joan moved to New York so that I could help with the records and Leiber and Krebs could manage her. Somewhere in there Krebs decided that punk artists were Nazis. If you remember back then they used to wear a lot of the Nazi armbands and Krebs didn't want any part of that. Joan is the most 'PC' person alive, and you never have any kind of racial epithet out of her ever. So it was kind of ironic, but they decided they weren't going to get involved.

"So I had this artist with no manager. We went to a couple of really big-name managers you would have heard of and each one did something nasty. One I went to with a great cover idea—"Do You Want To Touch Me"—and the guy stole the idea. In the end we overcame that. We went out to radio ourselves and told everybody the story and Joan's version was the one they went with. And while we were trying to find Joan a manager, suddenly we had a number-one record with 'I Love Rock N Roll,' and I was the manager. Since then I managed The Kinks for a few years and Darlene Love, who fell on some hard times and we helped her get back on her feet and got her in the *Lethal Weapon* movies series. Now she has a television show which she actually got from our office. And that's how I became a manager—by accident.

"While we were trying to find a manager, Joan was being rejected by every label in the business, so we printed our own records. We created a touring base for her. When she played around the Northeast they were having to close highways. It was like Woodstock every time. Something really great was happening. Now, a lot of it was circumstantial—a lot of it was that we made some good moves. I never thought it was because we were so great. At that time, having your own label was unique. Nobody was doing it. Why did we do it? Because I had a record that we recorded, and nobody would put it out. That's why we did it. It wasn't as if I had this genius vision, 'Oh, we could be an indie at this time and place,' but radio was unhappy with what the major labels were putting out, and within a blink, we had fifty major stations playing our indie record.'"

Q: What do you do day-to-day as a manager?

"We try to keep all our artists on good financial footing. If any of them are making money, I try very hard as a priority to put money away for them so they can maintain their dignity after their career gets cold because inevitably your career will get cold. That's my firm belief. You've got to assume that there's only going to be one or two Sinatras, and even Sinatra had a bad period! If Sinatra didn't get *From Here to Eternity*, who knows what would have happened to him because he was over. Neil Diamond was king of the world for ten years and he got cold. If you don't make arrangements to survive, you're going to have an undignified ending. We know guys who were lead singers in hit bands who are now doormen. While there's nothing wrong with being a doorman, it can be crushing for an artist. I was in Tommy James and the Shondells, and I was with Tommy once, and somebody came up to him and said, 'Didn't you used to be Tommy James?' It's a bad place to go."

Q: What do you like most about your job?

"I've had some good artists, right? You can't get a better artist than Joan Jett, and that's unique. So what do I like about it? She appreciates what I do. That's unusual, you know. Did I like managing The Kinks? Yeah. It was awesome. A lot of frustrations because there's a deep-rooted history there. There are two brothers and there were difficulties, but to be able to be the guy who's helping make career decisions for Ray Davies and Dave Davies is unbelievable. So that's satisfying as well, to guide awesome careers. To be the manager who brought them into the Rock and Roll Hall of Fame—that was incredibly gratifying.

"My favorite thing as producer, songwriter, or manager is to hear our records on the radio because when you start with a germ of an idea, a song that's being written, and it evolves into a record that evolves into a release that you can actually look at and finally you hear it on the radio—that to me is the number-one most satisfying thing. It's beyond the money and be-yond everything else. When these records start going on the radio, it's unbelievable."

Q: What do you find most challenging about the job?

"The number of crazy people that I have to deal with, includ-ing myself. You're dealing with subjugating the egos to try to keep the focus on the goal. To remain goal-oriented is the hard-est thing because there are so many personalities, and it's so easy to get emotional. I think maintaining the focus is the hardest thing and keeping the big picture in the front of your mind."

Q: What skills does one need to be an artist manager?

"Business skills are very important, as well as negotiating skills. There are different kinds of managers. I have certain guys we work with here who are associates or partners. Some of them are better at business than I am. I'm not bad at it, but my best skill, which I think is really important, is that I can take a record and find a place for it in radio or in the market. For example, we did very well with Metal Church, who we man-age, and Metal Church reached a point where the major labels didn't really want to deal with them. So we created our own independent release and we found a way to get them onto the heavy metal charts.

"If I can take a Darlene Love and get her on the easy listen-ing charts, that's great. To be able to adjust and adapt is a very important skill, to fit the artist into the market. Your artist isn't always going to be in vogue. Also, you have to understand the record business and the touring business—two totally separate businesses. As I said, the best thing a manager can do for an artist is to protect his or her financial security because that is the place where artists are the weakest. They're all geniuses, but when they're hot, they don't ever realize that that year's income is not the rest of their lives. It's that moment."

Q: *What advice would you give to someone who wants to become an artist manager?*

"I'd tell them it's a dumb business, truly. Right now, the middle is out of the management business, and I think it's not a great time to be in it. If you want to look at the guy who's managing Pearl Jam, he's a happy puppy, right? But years ago you could survive with a middle act. Right now, with the baby bands, and even bands up to the middle, until you get to be the Chili Peppers, it's really hard to survive as a manager because you're paying a lot of expenses and your income flow is limited.

"For me, I don't believe this is a great way to make money right now. As a matter of fact, we're trying to concentrate more on the record end. We have a label here that we've put more emphasis on than the management. I really think that in the nineties, management is a super risky job, and I almost think that the people who fall into it by accident are the ones who are better off—like Frank DiLeo, who was the promotion man who got Michael Jackson all those hits and then Michael said, 'Would you be my manager?' That's a great way to get into the management business.

"But to start without a lot of money and try to struggle your way to the top—yes, it can be done and people are doing it—but it is a crowded field. You have to be ready to take a lot of punishment, a lot of negativity, a lot of rejection, and I really think that somebody has to want it so bad that they're ready for years of torture. Somebody who is self-financed, somebody who comes from a very rich family, then you've got a better shot. But when somebody's going to try to survive, it's brutal. I think you've got to have some other kind of income flow because it's like trying to win the lottery.

"It's like being an artist. At least the artist is the one who's singing. If nothing else, they say, 'You know what? I played a show tonight. I've played only two this month, but those two hours are almost worth it,' and I've been there. When you get on stage and you're performing your music, that has a certain gratification. For a manager, hopefully you can get some pleasure from that, but it's a different level. It's brutal to be a manager in the nineties."

CHAPTER EIGHTEEN

Entertainment Attorney

W orking as a music business attorney can be a lucrative and rewarding career for those with a flair for the legal and a love of music. Music business attorneys often play a crucial role in the careers of artists, songwriters, producers, and record labels. Entertainment attorneys such as Warner Bros. Records' David Altschul have risen to lead major record labels mostly due to their efforts in negotiating artists contracts, arranging company mergers, acquiring catalogs, etc. One of the greatest thrills for a music business attorney is to find new talent and serve as the catalyst for making someone a star. Entertainment attorneys often look for talent that they can "shop" to record labels in order to land a record deal. After landing a deal, the attorney will either take a percentage of the artist's advance from the record deal or in some cases take a percentage of the artist's income during the period of the contract in return for legal services.

Craig Gates, Entertainment Attorney

In the day-to-day operations of a record label, the attorney plays an important and ongoing role in the growth and success of the label. In my own company, Interhit, we rely heavily on our attorney Craig Gates. One of our main activities is licensing masters from foreign record labels for our compilation releases, and Craig's expertise in this area has proved to be invaluable.

Foreign licensing can be quite complicated and can involve subtle legal points that can make a big difference in a record company's profit margin in the long run. Craig has also helped Interhit to license its own releases overseas. Craig talks about his job and the world of music business law.

Q: How did you get started in entertainment law?

"During the summers while I was in law school, I worked for a music publishing company and a local concert promoter. Those two jobs gave me the experience I needed to get a job working for another music publisher—doing work in the business affairs department from the outside as a consultant. That led me into some consistent work for a major music publisher, and I also went ahead and became part of an attorney referral panel for a songwriting organization.

"At the same time, I went around and, through the contacts I had, let people know that I was looking for and doing work as a music attorney, and clients started to come in from that. So, I broke in because I worked during the summer for a couple of different music companies, which eventually led to contacts who turned into clients. Basically, I started my own practice that way and had to build from those people I originally made contacts with—breaking in basically by diving in head first into working for music companies.

Q: What skills and education does one need to become an entertainment attorney?

"On the education side, while in law school, you should definitely be taking courses in intellectual property and copyright, in particular. If you know before you're going into law school that you want to be an entertainment lawyer, you should look for a law school that offers specific courses in entertainment law. Usually, law schools will offer maybe only one course in entertainment law. It's a very good background and will give you a broad spectrum of case law and statutes that apply to practicing as an entertainment attorney, dealing with book publishing, dealing with film, television, music, and anything else related to employment issues, cases which deal with either specific statutes in California or New York for employment, as well as various case law on copyright law in particular.

"Regarding the skills that one would need, entertainment attorneys are mostly confronted with their clients face-to-face all the time. You don't do work in the backroom, in research as much as you would, say, in a litigation law firm. You spend less time doing research than you would normally do for large law firms. You don't deal with nameless and faceless corporations. You definitely need great interpersonal skills. Knowing how to handle people and, in particular, talent as opposed to companies. You should be able to relate very well to talent in the entertainment field—actors, writers, producers, musicians, composers, and, in particular, artists. It takes a particular skill to be able to handle not only the legal problems, but often the general problems that artists will have in the industry. So you almost have to be more than simply a legal advisor, but a career advisor.

"The skills that you need to be an entertainment attorney go beyond the technical–legal aspect and into the interpersonal aspect, understanding how people work and helping people out with career problems. A mentor attorney once told me that you almost have to be a psychologist or a therapist as well as an attorney to be effective."

Q: What exactly do you do?

"An entertainment attorney basically negotiates contracts, drafts contracts, reviews contracts on behalf of their clients, as well as gives advice in connection with transactions that the client may be involved with. Also, in the event they're confronted with someone possibly trying to sue them, advising them on settlements, approaching settlements, suggesting what might be the effect of particular courses of action that the client may take. So from day to day, you're on the phone a lot, negotiating, contacting people, trying to make contacts for your clients, trying to generate business for your clients. You're on the phone a lot trying to generate business for yourself, keeping aware of what's going on, reading up on the trades in order to keep in contact with what's happening, who's working where. You will obviously have various meetings, not only with clients, but with other parties, and the rest of the time you'll spend drafting and reviewing contracts."

Q: What do you like most about your job?

"What I like most about my job is that it varies from day to day. The swiftness of most deals in the entertainment industry guarantees that you will go through many different transactions in a short period of time, whereas typically with litigation, you handle one case over the span of sometimes years.

"It's completely different in the entertainment industry. Everything's new all the time. You have different kinds of transactions that can occur, as well as various difficulties that your clients can confront. That's what's very interesting—things are changing all the time. That's definitely what I like about what I do. You're constantly confronted with new arrangements and new conflicts and new matters to handle."

Q: What's the most challenging aspect of your job?

"The most challenging aspect is keeping up with the changes in personnel in the different record companies, publishing companies, and in the film and television industry. The other challenging aspect is, with so many new forms of media being introduced all the time, keeping up-to-date with the different parameters of deals, with different companies doing different new things. These are the challenges, as well as continually trying to get to better and better deals for your clients."

Q: How is being an entertainment attorney different from being an attorney in other fields?

"Primarily, the distinction or difference between entertainment law on the transactional side, which is what I do—transactions, contracts, negotiations—and litigation is matters that you handle tend to take a very long time until they're resolved or adjudicated. Also, with music or entertainment law, you have a focus on a particular field of law and deal with matters only confronted in that area as opposed to, say, business litigation, which may handle any and all forms of failed transactions—lawsuits, bankruptcies, and so on. Entertainment law is also different in the sense that it's a very narrow field."

Q: What advice would you give someone who wants to become an entertainment attorney?

"The first thing is don't wait until after you get out of law school to look for a career in the entertainment industry. Often times, law firms that will hire on new attorneys and who hire on associates out of law school will be choosing them from their summer associate programs. You should look to do summer internships prior to law school with entertainment companies and, while in law school, some associate programs with law firms. Try to work in the legal departments at major entertainment companies to position yourself so that you'll gain some experience in the entertainment industry as well as contacts in the entertainment industry who, if they themselves cannot hire you when you get out of law school, may know of someone or a company that is looking to hire someone. The key thing is to position yourself prior to graduation for being in a situation where you're able to use the contacts that you've made over those years and to be aware of positions that become available through your network of contacts."

CHAPTER NINETEEN

Music Press

S ome of the most rewarding behind-the-scenes jobs in the music industry are those in the field of music journalism. Writing for a music publication about the music that you love can be a great source of fulfillment and enjoyment if your background and interests lie in the area of journalism and music. Many music magazines and local and national newspapers offer opportunities for free-lance and staff writers. A job in music journalism can put one right in the thick of the music scene. Whether you're covering local bands for your college newspaper or reviewing records for a national magazine or interviewing famous artists, a music journalist is there where the action is. A music writer keeps close tabs on the latest trends and developments and can sometimes actually become a part of music history in the making. Often a writer will write about artists in the early stages of their careers only to see them make it big later on. Nothing can compare to the thrill of being there before it all happens or, for that matter, when it all happens. Opportunities for careers in music journalism can be found at your college newspaper, local and national newspapers, local and national music magazines such as *Rolling Stone, Spin, Urb, DMA, Billboard,* and many more.

Many who have training in English or writing may find a natural progression to writing about music. I earned a degree in English and found that my writing training and my interests in music led to my work as a free-lance writer for *Dance Music Authority* magazine (DMA)—the premiere U.S. dance music magazine. Fortunately, I had the opportunity to begin writing for the magazine in its early stages, and this work resulted in an eventual promotion to assistant editor of *DMA*. You may find an opportunity through a friend at school or you may find a magazine on a newsstand for which you would like to write. Don't be afraid to send a writing sample and then contact the publisher. You never know where it will lead. Of course, don't expect to land a job at *Rolling Stone* with little or no experience. As with every job in the music industry, you need to work your way up the ladder and gain the experience necessary to advance. But if you love to write about music, the possibilities are there for a long and happy career in music journalism.

You may even have the desire and the resourcefulness to start your own music publication. Many underground music magazines are started by young people seeking to publicize and write about the music they love. Whether it be alternative rock, country, or dance music, the opportunity to run a magazine—to be your own boss—can be a tempting challenge.

Gary Hayslett, Editor and Publisher

DMA Editor and Publisher Gary Hayslett took this challenge in 1993 when he started his own music magazine—*Dance Music Authority*. In the past three years, *DMA* has grown to be the leading dance music publication in the United States. Gary's success story is an inspiration for others who want to break into the field of music journalism.

Q: How did you break into the business?

"In my late teens, it was the disco era and I started going to clubs. And even though I always had this passion for music, I took a regular job and worked for a regular company, Osco Drug. Eventually, I went into management and then started writing for a magazine called *Dance Music Report*. I liked it a lot, and when it folded I decided it was time to make a career change and start my own publication. I started *Remix Service Authority*, which covered reviews of remix services only and after *Dance Music Report* folded, there was a void in the marketplace for a dance music publication, so *Remix Service Authority* expanded to include dance music reviews, artist interviews, etc. So, *Remix Service Authority* became *Dance Music Authority*."

Q: What skills and/or education does one need to make it as a music journalist?

"In school I took business writing, so I didn't really go to school for this. I would encourage anybody who wants to write for a music publication or to start his or her own music publication to take journalism—take as many classes as you can, both business and creative writing.

"You also need really good interpersonal skills because you have to get people to do interviews, to deal with difficult people, to be persistent when people don't want to work with you, to smooth things over when you ruffle feathers on a bad review. So interpersonal skills are really important. Also, the ability to meet deadlines is critical."

Q: What exactly do you do?

"My job is a publisher/editor of the magazine. It's unique. Usually there's a publisher and an editor, but in my situation, I'm both the publisher and the editor. I handle coordinating all the reviewers, all the feature writers, lining up stories, topics, editorials, feature stories; lining up the advertising; coordinating the actual design and layout of the magazine; hiring the printer who prints it, the typesetters and layout people; following up on deadlines—everything. So when you're a small publication, you have to do more until it starts to prosper."

Q: And what do your writers do?

"We have what are called feature writers like Jeff Johnson who do artist interviews. Sometimes we do stories that aren't actual interviews—stories on specific topics. Then we have columnists who cover specific genres of music, and we have reviewers who write specific reviews about one song or one particular album. So it's up to them to get the music, critique it, and turn in their reviews.

"Most of the writers who write for us are free-lance writers; they don't write for us exclusively. We do have some people who write only for us, but for the most part they're all basically free-lance writers, which means they can write for whomever they want."

Q: What do you like most about your job?

"Probably the best thing is the freedom. You can work all hours of the day or night. When you work for a company, typically you're accountable for when you start and when you end. You have to work a set number of hours. If you're on a salary job, it usually means you work one and a half times as many hours as you're actually getting paid for. For example, when I worked at Osco, we got paid for forty-eight hours, but they thought you should work at least sixty or seventy hours. Having a magazine you get to meet a lot of people, go to a lot of cool places. It's a lot of work, but there are many benefits, mainly freedom to work at your own pace."

Q: What's the most challenging aspect of your job?

"Probably getting each issue out every month on time. You know we have to coordinate between twenty and thirty contributors in every issue, and that in itself is a challenge. Then there's the coordinating of the advertising. If we have forty ads in an issue, each ad requires three to four calls—first solicitation, follow-up, follow-up to deadline, follow-up after deadline. Then there's a follow-up for payment on the ad. So every facet has special challenges to it."

Q: What advice would you give someone who wants to write for the music business?

"I would encourage anybody who's in college, no matter what you want to do when you get out, to research all you can about the profession that you're thinking about going into. You want to make sure that, when you graduate from college, you have a degree in something specific, whether it's accounting, journalism, being a doctor or a nurse, whatever. Too many people go to college and they don't know they want to do and they take business classes or they take marketing classes and all that means is that you're going to end up in fast food or retail, the service industry, because all of those degrees mean just about nothing. You don't start out of school in a marketing job. What that entails is you're an assistant manager at some little store, fast-food chain, or whatever. If you want to write for someone or you want to do it for a career, you should specialize in that in school and then minor in something else, but go to school specifically for what you want to do, so you have that background to do it when you get out. Don't only take general classes."

Q: What's the best way to break in to music writing?

"Probably the best way is to send samples. Call the publication, tell them that you're going to send samples. Don't even call them and ask them 'How do I become?' Just send a package. The more you show initiative, the more you're going to get noticed. The people who call and hound on the phone are usually the laziest. All they do is waste your time. So don't talk about what you're going to do, just do it. Show somebody 'This is what I can do' and you'll get noticed a lot faster than the people who just want to talk about it. Take the initiative and send a package that shows, 'Hey, I'm a go-getter. Maybe you're not looking for people at the moment, but, if you are, this is what I can offer.'"

References

David Baskerville. *Music Business Handbook & Career Guide*. 1995.

Cardinal Business Media. *Recording Industry Sourcebook*. 1996.

Clevo & Olsen. *Networking in the Music Industry*. 1993.

Mark Halloran. *The Musician's Business and Legal Guide*. 1991.

Gary Hustwit. *Releasing an Independent Record*. 1995.

Cindy Laufenberg. *Songwriter's Market*. 1996.

Donald Passman. *All You Need To Know About the Music Business*. 1994.

James Riordan. *Making It in the Music Business*. 1991.

Diane Rapaport. *How To Make & Sell Your Own Recording*. 1992.

Shemel & Krasilovsky. *This Business of Music*. 1990.

Barbara Taylor. *National Directory of Record Labels & Music Publishers*. 1994.

VGM CAREER BOOKS

VGM Career Horizons
a division of *NTC Publishing Group*
4255 West Touhy Avenue
Lincolnwood, Illinois 60646–1975